EDEL QUINN

Edel Quinn
1907-1944

Desmond Forristal

DOMINICAN PUBLICATIONS

First published (1994) by
Dominican Publications
42 Parnell Square
Dublin 1

ISBN 1-871552-37-0

Cover design by
David Cooke

Printed in the Republic of Ireland by
Colour Books Ltd, Baldoyle, Co. Dublin.

Contents

Introduction

Edel Quinn died in Nairobi on 12 May 1944. She died far from her native country in a world at war. Her death was little noticed at the time except by her fellow members of the Legion of Mary. There were many other items to claim the newspaper headlines in Ireland and abroad.

The fifty years since her death have seen an extraordinary growth in the fame and reputation of this young woman. Soon after the end of the war, Frank Duff, the founder of the Legion of Mary, decided that her life-story was one that deserved to be more widely known. He invited Bishop (now Cardinal) Léon-Joseph Suenens to undertake the task of writing her biography. The bishop accepted, came to Ireland, met many of her family and friends, and brought back to Belgium a suit-case full of documents.

The book was published in 1953 under the title *Edel Quinn, A Heroine of the Apostolate*. Its success was immediate. It was translated into numerous languages and read throughout the world. It was the story of a young woman, suffering from terminal tuberculosis, who left the sanatorium and devoted her last few precious years to missionary work. It caught the imagination of millions. Many saw her as a saint for our times.

Calls for her canonisation became more widespread and more urgent. The official process was opened in Nairobi in 1963. A total of two hundred and fifty-eight witnesses gave evidence about her in Nairobi, in Dublin, and in seventy other locations in five continents. All these testimonies were sent to Rome, where the case for her canonisation is still under consideration.

As we approach the fiftieth anniversary of her death, the time seems ripe for a new biography of Edel Quinn. Since the publication of the book by Cardinal Suenens, many new facts about her have come to light, especially as a result of the canonisation process. Furthermore, there were aspects of her life that the Cardinal had to pass over in silence in order to protect the feelings and reputations of people still living at the time. It is hoped that the present work will present her as effectively to the people of our day as his did to the people of forty years ago.

In his recent autobiography (*Memories and Hopes*, Dublin, Veritas, 1991), Cardinal Suenens recalled the writing of his book on Edel Quinn. He commented on the fact that the canonisation process has been held up for lack of a miracle. 'For me,' he wrote, 'the miracle of her life is quite sufficient.'

ONE

The Bank Manager's Daughter

If a woman born in Cork is a Corkwoman, then that is what Edel Quinn was. Her birth took place on the 14 September 1907 at a place called Greenane, near the small town of Kanturk in Co. Cork. Her father, an official of the National Bank, happened to be stationed at the time in the bank's Kanturk branch. Within a year, the family had moved and there is no evidence that Edel ever visited Cork again. Still, the undisputed fact is that she first saw the light of day in Cork and must therefore be accounted a Corkwoman.

Neither of her parents came from Cork. Her father, Charles Quinn, was born in the town of Tuam in Co. Galway on 12 November 1871. His parents were William Quinn and Elizabeth Egan. As a young man he joined the staff of the National Bank, which had branches all over Ireland. He was working in the branch in Roscommon town when he met his future wife, Louise Burke Browne. Louise was a few months older than him, having been born in Kilmihil, Co. Clare, and baptised in the parish church there on 13 June 1871. She was the youngest of the seven daughters of Edmund Browne, a well-to-do farmer, and his wife Elizabeth O'Reilly.

Soon after his marriage to Louise Burke Browne, Charles Quinn was appointed to the bank in Kanturk. He moved there with his new wife and it was during their short stay there that Mrs Quinn gave birth to her first child, Edel.

Four days later the child was taken to the little stone church in nearby Castlemagner to be christened by the parish priest, Father F. H. Greene. It was the custom at the time to have the baptism as soon as possible after the birth, with the result that the mother was rarely present.

The absence of Mrs Quinn explains the confusion that attended the ceremony. Between them, Father Greene and Mr Quinn managed to frustrate all the mother's wishes. In the first place, they entered her name wrongly: the register records her as Louisa Bourke instead of Louise Burke Browne. More seriously, they gave the wrong name to the baby.

In a letter written twenty years later, Edel gave an account of the mishap. She was complaining about someone who insisted on calling her Edelweiss, a name she disliked intensely.

> I can remember only one person who ever called me my full name; and I know I hated her like poison. It is too long for one thing; I have not known anyone else with that name, as a matter of fact it was a mistake I was called it. Mum wanted me called Ada after a favourite sister of hers. The sister was often called Adele as a pet name. Mum told Papa when I was going to get christened to call me after Adele. Papa thought Mum meant Adele and told the priest and the latter said, 'Oh the name is of course Edelweiss, Edel for short.' So Edelweiss it was and Edel for always.

For the rest of her life, Edel was never quite sure whether her name was Edel or Edelweiss, whether she was called after an aunt or a small white Alpine flower. Though she always signed herself Edel, she could never entirely shake off the feeling that her real name was Edelweiss.

Once when writing to thank a friend for a gift of some holy pictures she added rather ruefully, 'I think you would have some hunt to find a St Edelweiss.' The rest of her family had no doubt that she was called after her aunt and always pronounced her name with the accent on the second syllable, sounding the same as Adele.

During the next ten years, Edel was to live in five different towns and acquire three sisters and a brother. Leslie was born in 1909 and Ralph, the only boy, in 1911. Then came Mona in 1914 and Dorothy, who for some reason was always known as John, in 1915.

The first move was to Clonmel, a prosperous market town in the nearby county of Tipperary. The Quinns went there a few months after Edel's birth and remained until 1913. When the time came for

Edel to start her education, her parents enrolled her in the local Convent school, which was under the care of the Loreto Sisters.

The Quinn home was a typical Irish Catholic home of the period. The parents had married comparatively late in life, which was common enough at the time, especially in the provinces. Both of them were faithful in the practice of their religion, and Mrs Quinn tried to attend Mass every day whenever possible. They provided their children with a secure and happy home life and passed on to them their own strong religious beliefs.

Mr Quinn was an easy-going, good-humoured man, who enjoyed a drink and a flutter on the horses. His career in the bank was one of steady if unspectacular progress. A photograph of him taken about 1920 shows a stoutish man of medium height, with bald head and heavy moustache. He is wearing a three piece suit, holding a walking stick in his left hand, and puffing on a pipe. He looks what he is, a prosperous bank official and a pillar of middle-class rectitude and responsibility. The photograph gives no hint of the weaknesses in his character that were shortly to bring disgrace upon himself and his family.

Mrs Quinn was a more intense and emotional type of person. Her photographs show her as a slightly-built woman with a sharp thin face. Despite her appearance, she had considerable strength of mind

Mr Quinn with Edel and Ralph, about 1920.

and body. She needed that strength when the family had to face the
crisis brought about by her husband's failings. Edel inherited her
strength of character as well as her deep piety.

The strongest influence on her in her childhood and youth was
undoubtedly her mother. The earliest surviving photographs of Edel
herself date from her Clonmel days, both of them taken when she
was four years old. One of them is a snapshot of her in a garden,
wearing dress and pinafore and high-laced boots and accompanied
by a large dog. The other is a studio portrait, the first and most successful of many. She looks full-face at the camera, with an amused
half-smile on her lips, a child obviously at peace with herself and
with the world around her.

In 1913 Mr Quinn was appointed manager of the bank in Cahir.
With his family, he made the ten-mile journey to his new place of
work. Though Cahir was a smaller town than Clonmel, the move
was an important promotion. The position of manager brought with
it many benefits. It recognised him as a rising man in the world of
banking, it gave him a substantial increase in salary, it provided him
with a comfortable rent-free home over the bank premises in the
town's central square. Furthermore, it marked him out as a person of
importance, with an assured position in the rigid hierarchy of Irish
small-town life. As befitted his position, he enrolled Edel in the private school run by the Sisters of Mercy in the town. In that class-
conscious age, many Irish convents had a small private school in addition to the national school which catered for the majority of the

*Mrs Quinn, with Edel and the
younger children, 1914*

pupils. Well-to-do parents were happy to pay extra fees so that their children could have the benefit of smaller classes and more select classmates. In Cahir, these included the children of some British army officers stationed in the area.

Edel's teacher was Sister Dympna, who prepared her for her first Confession and Communion. Her mother attended Mass every day and used to take Edel with her, giving her the foundation of a habit that was to last her all her life. She received her First Holy Communion in the parish church on Ascension Thursday, 1 June 1916. No photos of the occasion survive, but she is described as looking angelic in her white dress and veil, with her long golden hair falling almost to her waist.

The angelic look went hand-in-hand with a decidedly impish temperament. She soon established herself as the leader of her little group in the school. Vivacious and high-spirited, she was always involved in good-natured pranks and mischief. A favourite haunt was the convent bakery, where she was sure of a warm welcome from Sister Elizabeth. She would get a handful of currants from Sister Dympna and bring them with her to make a currant bun. One day

Edel. aged four

there, after she had been told for the umpteenth time to be good, she made the memorable announcement, 'I'll be bold, and I'll be bold always, and I'll never be good.' It was one promise that she failed to keep.

The next move for the family came in 1917 when Mr Quinn was appointed manager in Enniscorthy, Co. Wexford. Enniscorthy is a picturesque town, clinging to the side of a steep hill overlooking the River Slaney. It is the cathedral town of the diocese of Ferns and among its buildings is the handsome cathedral designed by the eminent English architect, Pugin.

Edel's new school was the Loreto Convent in Enniscorthy. Mother Thomas Aquinas, one of the teachers there, became a good friend of the family. She has left us a description of Edel which shows she had changed little since her time in Cahir.

> She was a real imp at school, not indeed bold, but always bubbling over with good spirits, full of life and gaiety and up to every kind of prank. She was the centre of every group bent on fun or mischief. A daring cyclist, often when dashing down the hill

Edel, aged 11, in Enniscorthy.

which leads from the convent to the town she used to turn round and wave, in order to show she was fully in control.

It was in Enniscorthy Cathedral that she received the sacrament of Confirmation on 27 October 1918. She took as her confirmation names Josephine Eucharia. The reason for her choice is not known, but it is likely that the first name was in honour of St Joseph and the second a sign of her increasing devotion to the Eucharist.

Her mother did not enjoy good health during much of the time in Enniscorthy. Labour was cheap and the Quinns could afford to keep two servants, a maidservant to do the cooking and cleaning, and a nursemaid to look after the children. Yet somehow or other, the family came to rely more and more on Edel, young though she was. She gradually began to fill the vacuum left by her mother's ill-health and her father's amiable inertia.

She began the day by going to the younger children's room and saying their morning prayers with them. Then she went with her mother to the 7.30 Mass in the Cathedral. After returning home for a quick breakfast she set off for school, walking or running so briskly that the girl from the house next door could never keep up with her. Back again after school, she would give her father some much-needed exercise by bringing him for a walk with their two dogs. Then it was time for her to supervise the children's evening prayers and lead them in the rosary. It is not surprising that the maidservant described her as a 'little mother'.

In the summer of 1921 Mr Quinn was appointed manager of the National Bank in Tralee. It was a further step up the ladder, as Tralee was the county town and administrative centre of Co. Kerry. The family settled into their new home over the bank premises in Denny Street and in September the girls were enrolled in the schools run by the Presentation Sisters.

Edel was by now well used to these changes and she was soon at home in her new school. One of her contemporaries there remembers her as 'a vivacious girl, always happy and smiling, but inclined to have head-colds quite often.' Her mother attended the 8 o'clock

Mass in the Dominican Church every morning and Edel presumably accompanied her. In the evening mother and daughters usually went for a walk out the Blennerville Road. It was the period of the struggle for independence in Ireland, and the daily newspapers were filled with reports of attacks and counter-attacks. These events seem to have left little mark on the tranquil life of the Quinn family.

In the summer of 1923 Edel was approaching her sixteenth birthday and her parents decided to send her to a finishing school for the last two years of her secondary education. A finishing school was an establishment, usually residential, which aimed at teaching social graces and deportment in addition to the normal school subjects. Its object was to turn girls into young ladies. Such schools were expensive but Edel was an attractive and talented girl and her father wanted to give her the best education that money could buy. Accordingly she was enrolled as a pupil in Upton Hall, Cheshire, a well-known English convent school not far from Liverpool. The school was under the care of the Faithful Companions of Jesus.

Edel arrived in Upton in September 1923. She was just sixteen years of age. It was her first time to be away from her home and family. If she was lonely, she gave no sign of it. She made friends

Edel at Upton, aged 16.

quickly, first among the nine or ten Irish girls in the senior school, then among the whole student body. In later years, she always spoke with affection and gratitude of her time in Upton Hall.

Her class mistress, Mother Philomena Hartigan, had a strong influence on the impressionable girl. In some letters written four years later, Edel described her as a broad-minded woman with a very attractive personality, who had made many changes for the better in the school.

She was newly appointed the term I arrived and she had only returned from 20 years in Australia and was Irish and this proved a bond. Then there were a few girls in the school who had a very bad spirit and they were spoiling everything, as most of the girls were not strong enough to stand out against them and found it easier to follow their lead. These thought they could carry on just the same under her rule but they reckoned without their host, and she would not tolerate any nonsense, and let them see it; these girls made everything unpleasant for a while but gradually the spirit died out and when one or two of the ringleaders left, the atmosphere was completely altered. It is extraordinary how great an effect one or two with wrong ideas can make on a number. I was in the form she had most to do with in the way of lessons etc, and so knew what she went through so that is how we were such friends.

It is in Upton that we first begin to see the mature Edel. She still has the vivacity and charm of her younger days, but these are now allied with a cool understanding and courage. To the teachers she was obedient and loyal though without any hint of servility. When blamed, even in the wrong, she was not concerned to defend herself. She was a solid and intelligent student, always near the top of her class. She was a keen athlete and distinguished herself on the hockey field and the tennis court. Her popularity with teachers and pupils was tinged with something very close to respect.

Her devotion to the Blessed Virgin grew and deepened in the

congenial atmosphere of the school. She had many opportunities to express it in the novenas for the Marian feast-days, in the October and May Devotions, in the Sodality of Our Lady of which she was a dedicated member. She became President of the Sodality, one of the highest honours the school could pay her.

One unhappy incident connected with the Sodality was recalled by a school friend of hers. There was an odd custom whereby the girls wore white veils at devotions during May, but those who had any mark against them had to wear a black veil. To everyone's amazement, Edel was given a bad mark for some unknown reason and was made to wear a black veil. She was deeply hurt but did not complain. But the rest of the school complained loudly and were in a state of near revolt over the incident. They blamed a nun who disliked her because she refused to justify herself when attacked. All ended well when Edel as Sodality President was given the honour of crowning the statue of Our Lady at the end of May.

An immeasurably greater blow was shortly to fall. Out of the blue, word came from Ireland that her father had suffered a business reverse and could no longer keep her at Upton Hall. The nuns may have wondered what kind of business reverse could befall a bank manager but they were given no details. Edel received the bad news with her customary composure. She said her goodbyes, packed her bags, and was brought by the nuns to the railway station at Chester, where she caught the boat train for Ireland. Her education was brutally cut short, her girlhood was at an end, she was now a woman. It was July 1924 and she was still two months short of her seventeenth birthday.

The disaster that struck the Quinn family in the summer of 1924 is still obscure though the main outlines are now known. At the time the family conducted a vigorous and successful cover-up campaign which they continued for many years. They managed to keep the details out of the biography of Edel written by Cardinal Suenens. This came from an understandable desire to protect their father's reputation and the honour of the family name but it made it impossible to understand much of what was happening to Edel at this time.

The fact was that Mr Quinn's hobby of betting on horse-races had by this time become a compulsion. There has always been a tradition in Irish business life of covering up for the faults of a colleague. No doubt his friends in Tralee and perhaps in previous postings as well had done all in their power to conceal his growing addiction. But there is a limit to what can be concealed. His gambling debts were mounting inexorably as he tried to recoup previous losses by increasing his bets.

The decision to bring Edel back from Upton had a two-fold purpose. The first was to save the large amount of money that would otherwise go on her school fees. The second was to have the help and support of this sixteen-year old girl who in a strange way was already beginning to be recognised as the real head of the family. Even her father deferred to her authority. He used to address her as 'Granny', an odd mixture of affection and respect.

This was the situation that faced her when she returned to Tralee in that fateful July of 1924. It was bad enough but there was worse, much worse, to come. It transpired that Mr Quinn, in an increasingly desperate effort to pay his debts, had been using bank money for gambling. In effect, he was robbing his own bank. He was guilty not just of folly but of crime.

The irregularity may have been discovered through the bank's own accounting system, or it may have been confessed by Mr Quinn. In any event, it could not have remained hidden for long. The question now was what would happen to the culprit. It was obvious that at the very least he would lose his managership and the house that went with it. It was also open to the bank to report the matter to the police in which case he would face trial on a charge of embezzlement and possibly incur a prison sentence.

One can imagine the anguished family conferences behind the lace-curtained windows in Denny Street, the pleadings in the manager's office with the men from headquarters, the prayers said and candles lit and Masses offered for a very special intention in the Dominican Church. In the event, Head Office did not seek its full pound of flesh. There were many factors that must have influenced the decision. There was Charlie Quinn's long record of service to the bank, there was his reputation as a basically decent if somewhat ineffectual man, there was the sad future facing his wife and young family. There was also the danger to the bank's own reputation. In the then highly competitive world of Irish banking, it would do the National no good to advertise the fact that one of their senior managers had been found with his hand in the till.

The verdict was finally pronounced. Mr Quinn was to lose his job as bank manager and leave the house in Denny Street. He was to be transferred to the bank's head office in College Green, Dublin, as what was called a 'ledger clerk', one of the lowliest posts in the banking hierarchy. No legal action would be taken against him. His salary was cut drastically and his career was at an end, but he still had his name and his reputation. His family could continue to hold up their heads as the family of a bank manager who had retired for reasons vaguely connected with health.

TWO

Love Story

The new home for the Quinn family was no. 22 Trafalgar Terrace in the Dublin suburb of Monkstown, a pleasant residential area on the south side of Dublin Bay. The houses in Trafalgar Terrace, built in the first half of the nineteenth century, faced the sea and commanded a view right across the bay as far as Howth Head. No. 22 was designed on a generous scale, a four-storeyed house with spacious rooms and high ceilings and an imposing flight of steps leading up to the front door. It was intended for a prosperous Victorian household with a staff of servants. But the number of families who could afford to live in such splendour was diminishing, and some of the houses in the terrace were being converted into flats. One of these was no. 22, where the Quinns rented the flat on the second floor.

It was rather cramped but it had its advantages. It was what was called a good address, a respectable house in a respectable neighbourhood. It was convenient to shops, schools and churches. It was close to Seapoint Station, from which regular trains ran to Dublin. It was just across the road from a popular bathing place, where Mrs Quinn got into the habit of having a swim every morning, winter and summer, before going to Mass. It was still possible for the family to keep up appearances as if nothing had really happened.

Still the first months of 1925 were difficult. The seven members of the Quinn household had to be fed and clothed on a greatly reduced salary. In addition the children had to be educated. Leslie, Mona and Dorothy were sent to the Dominican Convent school in Sion Hill, Ralph to Blackrock College, run by the Holy Ghost Fathers.

Edel went to commercial college. It was essential that she get a job as soon as possible and contribute to the family income. She went first to Potter's College in nearby Dun Laoghaire, then to

Rosse College in St Stephen's Green in Dublin. She learnt easily and quickly, mastering the necessary skills of shorthand and typing with no apparent difficulty. In the meantime, unpaid bills were mounting up at home and it was a struggle to keep food on the table. The sooner she started earning the better.

She sat the examination for the Irish Civil Service, but failed to secure a place. She was let down by her weakness in the Irish language, which had been neglected during her time in Upton. Then she heard of a vacancy in a small industrial agency in Nassau St, owned by Mr P. J. O'Hanlon. Many years later he described their first meeting.

> A friend told Edel Quinn that I was looking for a secretary and told her to apply. One Monday morning she knocked timidly at my door and I asked what had brought her here. I was greatly impressed by her modesty, by her open demeanour, by her prudence, and by the way she answered my questions. I didn't ask for any references. Her face was recommendation enough. I gave her the job. She used to do very confidential and responsible work, lodging and withdrawing money from the bank and suchlike.

Mr O'Hanlon was in his early forties at the time, a good-living and religious man. Some years later he decided to become a priest and was ordained for a diocese in England. During the year or so that Edel worked for him, his respect for her qualities increased steadily. He found he could leave her in complete charge of his office for a week at a time while he was away on business trips. His only concern was that he could not afford to pay her the wages that she deserved.

Among his clients was a young Frenchman who had come to Dublin to sell tiles. Pierre Landrin was twenty-five years old, energetic and active and with a good head for business. The two men got on well together and before long Mr O'Hanlon invited Pierre to become a member of the charitable organisation, the Society of St Vincent de Paul. He accepted the invitation and attended the weekly meetings faithfully. After the meeting, the two would visit the houses assigned to them in the Westland Row area of the city, giving help in the form of food and fuel and clothing. They would end their evening by having a cup of tea together.

Pierre's business entailed a large amount of paper work. One day, probably around the beginning of 1926, he asked Mr O'Hanlon if he could recommend someone who would make a good secretary. He suggested Edel for the job. He did not want to lose her but he knew that she was worth more than he was paying her and that she was the main support of her family at home. Pierre would make a good employer and could afford to pay a higher wage. In return, he would get the services of an extremely competent secretary. The two were introduced, each made a good impression on the other, the job was offered and accepted. Edel was now an employee of the Chagny Tile Company, Windmill Lane, Dublin.

Within a very short time, Edel had completely mastered the intricacies of the tile-importing business. Like Mr O'Hanlon before him, Pierre was amazed at her grasp, her efficiency, her judgement and her capacity for sheer hard work. He found he could leave the running of the firm to her for days on end with complete confidence.

But his relationship with her was not the same as her previous employer's. Mr O'Hanlon was a settled middle-aged man, who

Edel and her sister Leslie, with the foreman Mr Fagan, at the Chegny Tile Works, in 1927.

looked on Edel rather as a father would look on a favourite child. Pierre was in his mid-twenties, handsome, vigorous and vital. He saw Edel as something more than a model secretary. He saw her as a vivacious and attractive young woman, intelligent, charming and witty, with an impish sense of humour always bubbling away and a smile that lit up her whole face. 'She was always smiling,' he wrote later, 'and Edel Quinn's smile was something to remember; it was something bright and frank, wholly attentive and understanding; it shed light around her. Unconsciously, I must have grown used to that smile.'

It did not take long for a close friendship to develop between the two. This was helped by the fact that Pierre was lodging with a young couple, Dr and Mrs Taylor, whose home was not far from the Quinns. Pierre and Edel became part of the same set, meeting together, playing tennis together, dancing together. Something of the feel of those innocent carefree days comes out in an account written by Pierre many years later.

> When we played tennis at the Taylors' and it got too dark to see, we would sometimes go into the drawingroom, put a dance record on the gramophone, and then with Edel and Ethel Foley, Dr Taylor's sister, as partners, one or two young men and myself,

Pierre Landrin.

we used to dance. Vividly, I remember her as an incredibly lissom partner. To dance as she did – she was as light and as fleet as a sylph – she must have loved dancing.

Pierre saw her every day at work in the office, surrounded by accounts and ledgers. He saw her often in the evenings or at weekends, and came to know her parents and her family. When a vacancy for another typist arose, he gave the job to her second sister, Leslie. Yet there was a side of her life that was totally hidden from him.

He knew that she always arrived punctually for work but he did not know that she attended early Mass every morning, snatching an apple for her breakfast and running all the way to Seapoint station to catch her train: one of the regular commuters christened her the Seapoint Sprinter. He did not know that she made Sunday a day of prayer, with two or three Masses in the morning and devotions in the afternoon or evening. He did not know that she was one of the leaders in the Loreto Social Club, a club for girls from a poor area in the north side of the city. He did not know that she was an avid reader of religious books and was familiar with the writings of many of the great spiritual masters. He did not know that she felt drawn to the life of a contemplative nun and was planning one day to enter the Poor Clares. Forty years later he was asked how well he knew her and he answered, 'I knew her and I didn't know her at all.'

He could not help being aware of her deep faith, even though she hardly ever spoke about her religion. She was never one to indulge in edifying conversation or displays of piety. She enjoyed life, she dressed simply but elegantly, she was delightful company. Yet she gave the impression of being someone who lived her whole life unaffectedly in the presence of God.

One thing that struck him particularly was her extraordinary conscientiousness in carrying out her duties. She never came a moment late or left a moment early. There was one day when he kept her working all through her lunch break. When he realised what had happened, he told her to go for alunch. She refused, because she felt she should be at her post during official working hours. He ended by going out and bringing back cakes for her and being rewarded by one of her matchless smiles.

Gradually he began to examine his own life. For years religion had meant nothing to him: but now, under her unspoken influence, he returned to Mass and the sacraments. It was no passing fancy but a deep and permanent conversion. Through her he found a faith that was to remain firm and rocklike until the end of his life.

In the summer of 1927 he decided to leave Dublin and take up a position in London. He was by nature a wanderer and he had been six years in Ireland. It was time for a change. Before going, he wanted to see some of the beauty of the country so he went on a walking tour of County Kerry, starting from Ireland's most famous beauty-spot, Killarney.

One evening he arrived exhausted at the Great Southern Hotel in Parknasilla after a twenty-mile walk. It was too late to get a meal so he went straight to bed. He woke in the morning and found that his mind was filled by a single thought. He would soon be leaving Ireland and would never see Edel again. He realised with sudden and total clarity that he was in love with her and that he wanted her to be his wife.

He returned to Dublin and continued with the arrangements for his departure. Another French firm took over the Chagny Tile Company, retaining the by now indispensable Edel. Though not yet twenty years of age, she was appointed manager with a substantial increase in salary. During all this, Pierre said nothing to her about his feelings. Perhaps it was just a fancy that would pass. He left for London and started in his new job. But it was not a passing fancy. Distance did nothing to lessen his ardour. Every day convinced him more and more of his love for Edel. By chance he was given an opportunity of declaring himself. Some hitch developed in the transfer of the tile company and he was asked to visit Dublin and sort it out. He arrived back in Ireland towards the end of August, determined not to leave until he had told her of his love.

The opportunity came on 1 September 1927, a date that remained for ever imprinted on his memory. He invited Edel to be his guest for lunch. It was not to be the usual rushed affair but a leisurely meal in one of Dublin's principal restaurants. He chose Jury's Hotel in College Green, the heart of the city's financial district. There in the stately old-world dining room, he poured out his heart to Edel.

Her reaction was not what he had hoped for. She listened sympathetically, touched and flattered by his declaration, moved by his sincerity. But there was a sadness in her face that chilled him even before he heard her response. When she spoke at last, it was with great tenderness and openness. She assured him of her esteem and affection but said that she could never be his wife. She was promised to someone else.

For the first time, he heard from her the full story of her life. She told him all about the troubles in the home, about her father's gambling and his misuse of bank funds and the sad consequences that had followed. She was now the main support of the family and would continue to be so until the others were old enough to earn their own living. She herself had made up her mind to become a contemplative nun. She had already made arrangements to enter the convent of the Poor Clares in Belfast. She had promised to dedicate her life totally to God if her family was saved from public disgrace. It was a sacred promise and she would never break it. She asked him to understand her reasons and to forgive any pain she might have caused him.

It was a long and emotional encounter. Both of them were completely drained as they left the restaurant. Edel returned to her home and told the family that Pierre Landrin had asked her to marry him and that she had refused. For once her self-control deserted her and they were surprised to see that she was crying.

Pierre was even more affected. Years later he wrote, 'On the night boat that brought me back to Liverpool a few days later, the few passengers sitting late in the saloon saw a young man, his head bowed between his hands, giving tearful rein to his sorrow.' As soon as he got back to London, he wrote a letter to Edel. Her reply is dated 7 September 1927, just six days after the fateful lunch.

> Did you come in from Chislehurst to Westminster Cathedral?
> That must have meant a fairly long fast. How far was it from
> where you stay? I was at Communion also but the Church was
> Monkstown. I asked Our Lady to look after you, and do what is
> best for you, so I know you are in good hands. I know she will ob-
> tain something good for you, and far better than if she gave you
> what you want.
>
> Please do not say you are not worthy, Pierre, it is not true, you
> are far above me in every way. God knows that, and it is only His
> merciful love that could call me to serve him in religion, seeing
> what I am. Please pray for me that I may become a little less un-
> worthy of Him.

That is the only reference in a relatively long letter to what had
happened between them. The rest of it is devoted to family and business matters. It was to be the first in a long series of letters. He wrote
to her every week in French, she replied in English. They were letters that he read and re-read and treasured and brought with him
wherever he went and kept until the day of his death. It would have
been easier for her to let the correspondence die, but she obviously
felt a responsibility as well an affection for him.

His letters have been lost but hers are still preserved. They show
a rare maturity and judgement. She encourages him, advises him,
listens to his woes and tells him something but not everything of her
own. She offers him friendship and affection and support but she
never says anything that would raise his hopes or suggest that she
might ever change her mind. It is a thin line to tread but she treads it
unerringly. Gradually he became reconciled to the reality of their relationship, as a later letter of hers shows.

> Pierre, I am delighted that you see things from my point of view.
> Though I know my explanations were not very clear, yet this was
> from lack of proper expression, as in my own mind they were
> perfectly clear. I knew when you understood that I, however un-

worthy, have one love and one only, Our Lord, you would know that I would not change. I thank God He has made you understand this. It is a help when one can know and take a thing as definite. But it is not a sacrifice that one makes really to enter. One gives up something for a time, but one gains at the same time everything; it is a spiritual marriage.

I will not unfortunately be free to leave home, as I told you, for at least a year, and I shall of course tell you when the time comes, when we may join in thanking God for His graces. You will pray for me, I need prayers badly, and let us pray that in all things God's Holy Will may be done.

Several times he suggested making a return visit to Ireland. Each time she tried gently to dissuade him. He finally arrived in July 1928 and spent a week-end in Dublin. He and Edel attended a play in the Abbey Theatre and went on a trip to Bray, a seaside resort not far from the city. It was a pleasant couple of days, but no more than that. It must have convinced him that there was nothing he could do to change her mind. They never saw each other again.

The exchange of letters continued for several years. It died out in the early thirties, due largely to his habit of moving from country to country. He married eventually and had a son and two daughters, one of whom he named Edel. He died in France in 1980.

THREE

A Girl about Town

Edel's letters to Pierre tell us much about her activities during the next two years. They tell us less about her thoughts and her interior life. She was always a deeply private person and her prayer was something she shared only with her spiritual director. Still she could not help giving Pierre occasional glimpses of her spiritual journey, especially when she felt it might help and encourage him on his own way.

She usually signed her letters 'Very affectionately yours, Edel H.B.S.'. This led to a query about the initials. She explained that she was enrolled in the movement called Knights and Handmaids of the Blessed Sacrament, a movement aimed at increasing devotion to the Eucharist. 'The primary condition is weekly communion, this is essential, afterwards it is left to the individual to live up to his knighthood by assisting at Benediction and by visits etc.'

She made it gently but firmly clear to him that her decision to enter the convent was unalterable. At the same time, she revealed something of the resistance she had put up before accepting her vocation.

You see, Pierre, I have not changed my mind and, if it is God's will, I don't believe I ever will. I feel absolutely certain that I am doing what is God's will for me. This certainly sounds presumptuous, I know, when one considers the calling; but the call to the Religious Life is a grace from God, and when one receives it there is no mistaking it. One may be for years without the slightest inclination for such a life, and even feel a dislike for it, and yet when one gets the call, even though they fight against it and try to put away the thought, still it persists and one sees quite clearly what is God's will, and to act otherwise would be to do what one did not believe to be right and reject God's grace.

In October 1927, a few weeks after that day in Jury's, Edel returned to Upton Hall for a reunion of past pupils. She gives an amusing description of an Englishwoman with whom she shared a cabin on the voyage across the Irish Sea. 'She talked and talked and talked and when I did get to sleep she woke me up again at about 5 a.m. to tell me she was thinking how lonely her little white cat must be without her!! ... The funny part was that she casually mentioned she had left her little boy at school whilst she was on this 14 day holiday; all the time it was the cat she was fretting about for fear it would be lonely.'

She met many of her old school companions at the reunion. 'It is funny what a change three years make. Some of the girls had altered a great deal, one or two had acquired a rather bored expression and talked and looked at everything as if it wearied them and they wanted to get away, they seemed only half alive. I noticed they were mainly those ones who had nothing much to do with their time at home.'

She had some interesting comments to make about the life of the nuns who were teaching in the school.

One thing that struck me very much was the fact that the nuns have really so little time for prayer, not nearly so much as one would expect. For example, there is meditation early in the morning but the Class mistress is only present at Mass and then the whole community leave the Chapel about ten minutes after Mass (they have to, to fit in the classes), which seems very hard on them. There are classes all day and the nuns have about one hour free for 1. their early Exam of Conscience which is supposed to take about 15 minutes 2. their recreation. They have half an hour's Spiritual Reading, which all are not free to attend, and then their night visit to the Blessed Sacrament. So that their teaching hours and care of girls etc. comprise nearly the whole day. Then one can see that contact with the girls often causes them distraction through over-attachment. Of course their work is prayer, but wouldn't you think it very unsatisfactory to have so little time to really devote uninter-ruptedly to God, if one was a nun. This fact never dawned on me so forcibly as when I was free to go round during my week-end; and it struck me how difficult it was for them to be recollected when they were constantly coming in contact with different people, even girls; it seemed very hard on them to be so tied down, when they had left the world.

Her comments show why she had decided to enter a contemplative order rather an active one. Indirectly, they give a hint of the thirst for prayer that was beginning to become the mainspring of her life.

She plans to study French and Latin and asks Pierre for his advice, as he has knowledge of both languages. An improved knowledge of French would help her in dealing with the French owners of the Chagny Tile Company. Her reason for studying Latin is more interesting.

> You see, the Order I intend to enter is a Contemplative one, and the Divine Office, which is in Latin, is recited during hours of the day and night. The Mother Abbess asked me if I had ever done Latin and I said I had done some at school, but that my knowledge was anything but good. She said they had a nun who taught those who did not know Latin well, so that the Office would be intelligible to the reciter. On hearing this I decided it would be far wiser to take up the study at once, so as to give as much time as possible to getting a decent knowledge. I thought that if they found it helpful to start teaching one when one entered, then it would not be waste of time to begin now, no matter how absurd it appeared.

Books figure frequently in the letters. Pierre was a keen reader and Edel was happy to recommend some of her own favourites. She suggests that he pay a visit to a religious bookshop. 'I think if you start strolling round Burns and Oates you will become a good client. It is very difficult to resist buying books, I find.' She recommends the works of St Teresa of Avila and St John of the Cross and she mentions that she reads *The Imitation of Christ* every night before going to bed.

She frequently refers to writings by and about St Thérèse of Lisieux, the Little Flower, but she reacts strongly when he sees a resemblance between her and the saint. 'You know you don't know me at all, if you could even for a moment think such a thing; you know the Little Flower was a saint; and I am not even on the first step of the ladder!' In later years, many others were to remark the same resemblance.

Her reading includes writers from the English Catholic tradition. She speaks of the works of Francis Thompson and Coventry Patmore, and has a high regard for Newman, which she shares rather surprisingly with her father. 'Have you read many of Newman's books? I suppose you have read his 'Apologia'. My father is always reading and studying him and will discuss him for as long as possible on any occasion; and always takes any reference to Newman, in writings or conversations, as almost a personal compliment!'

When a young French employee of the firm professed to be an atheist, she thought at once of Newman. 'About the second day he was here, he said that he never knew any clever person who studied religious questions who adopted the Catholic Church as, apparently, intellectual people would not accept Mysteries and must have reasons. Then I asked him if he ever heard of Cardinal Newman, but he said No and cleared to his lunch.'

The affairs of the Tile Company naturally take up a large part of the correspondence. The office where she worked was a crude wooden structure set down in the middle of the yard and surrounded by tiles and other building materials. It was known appropriately as The Hut. It had no heating and was bitterly cold in winter. 'You will laugh when you hear I have two woollen jumpers on, two cardigans, my costume coat and my big coat and a scarf, and still I freeze.' It is strange that she never considered having a stove installed. It may have been a form of deliberate penance. The long-term effect on her health can only have been harmful.

Shortly after Pierre left, her salary was raised to two pounds ten shillings a week, more than double the usual rate for a girl of her age and qualifications. There is no doubt that she was worth every penny of it. When the foreman, Mr Fegan, was rushed to hospital with a perforated appendix, she took on his duties in addition to her own and did not leave the office until 7.30 or 8 most nights.

She had the ability to keep her head in a crisis and to stand firm when she believed she was in the right. Those who thought that a twenty-year-old girl could be easily intimidated soon found they had misjudged her. In May 1928 an error in Head Office resulted in an enormous delivery of tiles from France. 'The hut looks like an oasis in the desert, tiles, tiles everywhere.' This led to a dispute with the men who were unloading them.

> The men found it slow work to keep storing the tiles, especially when it came to placing them in bad corners, and they stopped work to get paid a day's pay for the extra day they found it necessary to work, i.e. Wednesday, instead of getting paid per ton only. They stopped work for two hours on Tuesday, at length we agreed to give a day's pay for Wednesday (today). When it came to pay them, we counted the 600t they had worked on till Tuesday night (and not the full 700t) plus a day's pay. They refused to accept this and claimed tonnage in full plus a day's pay and after arguing and arguing they went down to the Workers' Union. The latter gave no satisfaction to them, so they came back again and argued and finally cleared off without their money and said they would consult a solicitor tomorrow morning. But they are, I believe, in the wrong and any way you take it, as it is have the best of the bargain.

A postscript to the letter, written the following day, gives the ending to the story. 'We settled up with the men at 1 p.m. today! After spending from 11 o'clock arguing the point, they finally gave in; they might just as well have settled up when the boat finished yesterday.' It was a portent of things to come. A girl who at the age of twenty could face down a squad of angry Dublin dockers, was clearly destined for greatness.

Her responsibilities did not cease when she returned to her home in Trafalgar Terrace. Her father, whom she always refers to with affection, was quite content to let her take over the role of head of the family. When her brother Ralph began to get bad school reports from Blackrock College, it was Edel who was given the job of seeing the Dean.

As Papa has only Saturday free and hates interviewing either priests or nuns, and Mum is busy and also loathes such interviews, there is no one left except myself. The Dean is fairly young and has a most doleful way of speaking, like the younger priest in the Abbey play, he would really send you into the depths! He said Ralph could do well if he studied steadily and ordinarily, and said he would look to him and let us know how he would get on at Easter. I told him Ralph was probably going for the Bank so he said he'd have to work hard. Next day he asked Ralph was I the youngest girl of the family, how old I was, and finally said 'Are not sisters terrible bosses'!! However, whatever he thinks re my interference, I am going up at Easter to know the result.

She does not name the Dean in the letter. The Blackrock College records show that the Dean at the time was Father John Charles McQuaid. In 1940 he was appointed Archbishop of Dublin to the surprise of the priests of the diocese, who had not expected that a member of a religious congregation would be given the post. His low voice and rather forbidding manner were to be much imitated by the younger clergy.

At this period she was still enjoying a fairly active social life. Even though she was destined for the convent, she saw nothing wrong in principle with going to dances and parties. The qualities which had attracted Pierre attracted others as well and she had more than one proposal of marriage. She kept her suitors at a distance and was quick to react when wholesome fun seemed to take a turn in the wrong direction.

People in the Terrace gave an informal dance on Sunday night and Les and I were there. It was not very enjoyable as things were rather slow, and in the end they played games based on Postman's Knock; in case you don't know the latter it is briefly this:– all the men go out and the girls remain in the room, and then the latter get numbers. Each boy in turn is Postman and knocks at the door and mentions a number and the girl who has that number must give the Postman a kiss. Personally I think it stupid and cleared home before it began. Hide and Seek is all right and good fun but the other games are rotten. They danced the Yale a good deal and very little Charleston. The Yale is nice and is slower and more graceful than the Charleston. I think you'd like it.

The interest in new dances was very much part of the Twenties' culture. She and Pierre had mastered the Charleston while he was in Ireland. Now she sent him information about the latest craze. 'As a relaxation for you I enclose a copy of the "Instructions for Yale Blues"! It is the one we were using and we found it quite decent to follow; I have a copy so you need not worry about returning it. The Evening Herald is far ahead of Yale Blues and last time I saw the dancing instructions, they related to a dance newer than the Yale. So where is one?!!' Further information about the new dance was soon forthcoming. 'Les brought in today an instruction copy of a new dance "The Heebie-Jeebies". Beautiful name! Whether it will be danced or not is another question. So until we hear further, I think it is wisest to stick to the Yale.'

As the days lengthened into the summer of 1928, there was more talk about outdoor pursuits. Her mother swam in the sea every day. Her father and her sister Les were keen swimmers too and took part in competitions. She enjoyed swimming herself but her real love was tennis. A chance meeting on the train with her old employer, Mr O'Hanlon, led to an introduction to the secretary of the Clarinda Park Tennis Club in Dun Laoghaire. It was a small club with about forty members. Most of the girls were in their early twenties but there was a wider age-range among the men. Edel and her father became members. The subscription was £1 a year.

We had a tennis tournament that began at 11 and we finished at 10.30 p.m.! We had the usual mixed doubles to wind up with. Papa and his partner won the mixed and got 16/- and my partner and I won the ladies and got 4/-. The prizes were merely nominal as it is a social club and not wealthy! It was good fun though, especially

as the day was so lovely. My face is one red blob and it will be all
blisters tomorrow and the skin will peel off, the same with my neck
and arms, I know by experience; it is just like a burn.

July brought heat and sickness. In a letter written in pencil, she
admits that she is suffering from pleurisy and that the family has
insisted on her going to bed. A few days later she claims to be fully
recovered.

I got your letter this morning, I am A.1. now thanks, it must have
been an attack of 'Flu'. It was lucky it was not pleurisy, as I believe
it takes ages to get better of one type of it anyway. You have had
experience of it certainly. Of course I am made stay in bed late in
the morning and go to bed early at night like a baby at present, but
I am truly O.K.

There are no further references to illness. She does not say if she
was examined by a doctor. It seems unlikely that she contracted
influenza during a midsummer heatwave. It looks like the first sign of
the illness that was to take her life fifteen years later.

Her social and business activities are chronicled at length. Less
space is given to her religious activities, but scattered throughout the
letters are references to retreats, missions, novenas, triduums, Devotions and, of course, Mass. 'Yes', she writes, evidently in reply to a
question of his, 'I usually go to 7 Mass in Kingstown on week-days,
somehow there is always a terrible gap in a day when one misses Mass
and Communion.' On Sunday she goes to early Mass in Blackrock or
Monkstown with the family, then after breakfast goes into town to
attend further Masses in Clarendon St. 'It is very quiet and for the late
Masses there is a good choir, I think you'd like it.'

There is even less about her works of charity. Once she excuses her
delay in replying to a letter on the grounds that she had to visit a great-
aunt. 'Most of my evenings seem spent in seeing people, and as most
of the latter are old, I don't like disappointing them.' No furthers
details are given of the old people in question.

Another good work was the annual flag-day for the Society of St

Vincent de Paul. To someone of her sensitive disposition, selling flags in the street was an ordeal. 'Pierre, I have always marvelled how anyone could ever be a commercial traveller; I loathe asking a person for anything, or to do anything even when it is not personal, and I guessed the flag selling would not prove my 100% abilities.' Her good-humoured account of what happened should strike a sympathetic chord with all reluctant canvassers.

> On Saturday, another girl and I went into town at three and found sellers at Westland Row. We went down O'Connell Street to Earl Street; all along O'Connell Street, flag sellers were legion and everyone was flagged and beflagged. We kept on and worked up and down Earl Street, still the same story, and my companion, Eileen O'Carroll, a pal of Les's, got one penny. Seeing Earl Street was no use we decided to try Henry Street; same story but worse, each door of Woolworth's had 3 sellers. We worked up O'Connell Street by the Green to George's Street, and it also was well patrolled. I tried on the dodge you spoke of re the 'Young Couples', but invariably they both pointed to their coats, or worse still, if outside appearances raised hopes, they opened the top of coat to show a flag stuck inside, and not one had the decency to part a second time with money for the cause. So it is a jolly good thing Vincent de Paul is not counting on my collection for support. So so much for my powers of parting money from its owners!! Eileen and I ended up with tea at Robert's by way of consolation.

Only once does she talk about the work that was taking up an increasing amount of her time, the club in North Great George's Street. Again she was responding to a question from Pierre, who asked if the Handmaids of the Blessed Sacrament were involved in social work. No, she told him, but the Children of Mary Sodality to which she also belonged did have social work attached.

> There is a national school attached to the Convent in North George's Street, and as you can judge from the locality the children are desperately poor. All the work is done amongst them, such as

providing dresses for them and seeing to their Communion clothes, giving them entertainments and treats, and food and money. Of course, as the sodality is only in its infancy, there remains a geat deal to be done to work this properly and efficaciously; so far on several occasions jealousy on the part of some who were less poor amongst the parents caused a good deal of trouble, as they thought they were overlooked.

Next Sunday we are supposed to be giving them a treat; it was fun working out the fare for 640 children in proportion to the funds! Buns, oranges, sweets and prizes was the most that could be done; it was queer working out sweets by the hundredweight and oranges by cases. It lasts from 3 to 6, the competitions are chiefly dancing, recitation and singing. The only luck is that the whole 640 don't enter; as it is, the number who do is pretty stiff. It would require courage to act as adjudicator, it wouldn't be an easy job. Like the replies to your advert. for office boy, the applicants won't be over many.

Nowhere in the letters to Pierre does she mention the Legion of Mary. When their correspondence petered out in the spring of 1929, she had apparently not yet made the acquaintance of the organisation that was to dominate the rest of her short life.

FOUR

Meeting Mr Duff

Edel met Mona Tierney for the first time in the Loreto Convent in North Great George's Street. It was at a meeting of the Children of Mary. Ireland is a small country, and when two Irish people meet for the first time they usually try to find out if they have any acquaintances in common. They are rarely disappointed.

It turned out that Mona had been very friendly with Edel's uncle and aunt and cousins in the West of Ireland. Edel was delighted and immediately invited her to visit the home in Trafalgar Terrace and meet her mother. She suggested the following Thursday evening as a suitable date.

'I'm very sorry,' Mona said. 'Thursday is my Legion meeting.'

'Your Legion meeting?' Edel asked. 'What's that?'

She listened with interest as Mona told her about the Legion of Mary, an organisation of Catholic lay people which had been founded in Dublin in 1921. It consisted of a number of small cells, each of a dozen or so members, who met once a week to pray together and to undertake different forms of apostolic work. The cell (it was called a Praesidium) to which Mona belonged met every Thursday evening at eight and devoted itself to visiting homes in the North City area around the Loreto Convent, an area with which Edel was already familiar. Edel said, 'I'd love to join.'

Mona consulted Nancy Hogg, the president of the Praesidium, and told her that Edel wished to join. 'I'm not so sure the Legion will appeal to her,' she added in all honesty. On first acquaintance, Edel struck people as someone gay and light-hearted and attractive but lacking depth, a charming butterfly flitting over the surface of life, a Bright Young Thing who might have stepped out of the pages of Evelyn Waugh. Though Mona later came to know her well, there were parts of her personality that remained forever hidden. She was to say, in words that strangely echoed Pierre Landrin, 'In all fairness, I didn't know Edel. You know, I didn't know her depth.'

Mona's misgivings did not deter the president, Nancy Hogg.
'Bring her along,' she said.

The meeting of the Praesidium of Our Lady of Victories took
place the following Thursday at 8 p.m. in 6 Gardiner Place, just
around the corner from North Great George's Street. When Edel entered, she saw in the centre of the room a plain table surrounded by
chairs. At the head of the table, in the place normally occupied by
the chairperson, was a statue of the Immaculate Conception on a
white cloth. Flanking the statue were two lighted candles and two
vases of flowers. In front of the statue and a little to the right was a
curious object known as the vexillum. It consisted of a small globe
surmounted by a reproduction of the miraculous medal and the
words *Legio Mariae*. At the top was a dove with outstretched wings,
symbol of the Holy Spirit. Modelled on the standards of the Roman
legions, it was the standard of the Legion of Mary.

The meeting started punctually. Everyone knelt down for the
opening prayers, which consisted of an invocation to the Holy Spirit
and the five decades of the Rosary. Then they sat down, a short extract was read from a spiritual book, the minutes of the previous
meeting were read and signed, and the members started giving their
reports.

Many different kinds of apostolic work were open to the Legionary, visitation of houses, hospitals, prisons, making parish censuses,
bringing children to Mass, organising study circles, distributing
Catholic literature, promoting sodalities, caring for the altar and the
church, supporting the foreign missions, running hostels, clubs and
organisations of various kinds. The only work forbidden to them
was the giving of material aid. Apart from the fact that this was the
special field of the St Vincent de Paul Society, it was felt that giving
money or food might suggest that all houses where the Legionaries
called were receiving charity, resulting in their visits becoming un-
welcome.

The work of the Praesidium of Our Lady of Victories was mainly the visiting of the poor tenement houses in the neighbourhood. Gardiner Place led into Mountjoy Square, once the pride of Dublin's north side. Now the gracious Georgian mansions had fallen on evil days. Front doors hanging off their hinges opened on to halls filled with prams and street-barrows and empty packing cases. Rotting staircases with roughly patched banisters led to the basements or to the upper floors where whole families lived in single rooms, with as many as eight or ten families in one house. It was the area, thinly disguised as Hilljoy Square, in which Seán O'Casey set his famous plays about the lives of Dublin's slum-dwellers.

The first thing that struck a visitor was the abject poverty of the people. It was only later that their more positive attributes began to emerge, their humour, their warmth, their neighbourliness, their courage, their resilience, their deep religious faith. The reports of the Legion visitors were not the drab catalogue of human misery that might have been expected. There was hope and goodness and a surprising amount of laughter.

Towards nine o'clock the giving of reports was interrupted. Everyone stood and recited the *Catena Legionis*, the Chain of the Legion. It consisted of the *Magnificat* with an introductory antiphon and a concluding prayer. 'My soul doth magnify the Lord, and my spirit hath rejoiced in God my Saviour.' The *Magnificat*, Mary's great hymn of praise and thanksgiving, was the chain that held the members of the Legion together. 'He hath filled the hungry with good things, and the rich He hath sent empty away.' They praised a God whom they had met more often in slums and tenements than in the houses of the wealthy.

After the *Catena* came the *Allocutio*, a short spiritual talk given by the spiritual director or, in the director's absence, by the president. The giving of reports was resumed and the work for the coming week was allocated. Edel noticed that the members were called Brother or Sister. Her friend Mona was Sister Tierney, the president was Sister Hogg. She noticed too a small bag being passed around among those present. It was the secret bag into which they made their contributions for the running expenses of the Legion. Then they stood for the concluding invocations and prayer, a petition for faith, 'that fullness of faith in Thee and trust in her to which it is given to conquer the world.' The meeting ended in the name of the Father and the Son and the Holy Ghost.

If Edel had any doubts before, she had none now. It was, in her own words, love at first sight. She asked Sister Hogg if she could join the Legion and was accepted at once. There was a three months' probationary period before she was officially enrolled but she was allowed from the outset to attend the meetings and take part in the work. To all intents and purposes she was now a member of the Legion of Mary.

Visitation was normally done in pairs. Edel's partner for much of the time was Mona. The work took up a second evening of the week. Together Sister Tierney and Sister Quinn trudged the pavements, climbed the stairs, knocked at the doors of the people of Mountjoy Square and the neighbouring streets. They introduced themselves as members of the Legion of Mary, explained the nature and purpose of the Legion and asked for prayers for their work. They handed out pamphlets and prayer leaflets and holy pictures. They inquired about children and old people. They arranged for the priest to bring the sacraments to the sick or to consecrate the home and family to the Sacred Heart.

Sometimes they were rebuffed and a door was slammed angrily in their faces. They reported it at the next meeting and promised that they would try again. More often, much more often, they were greeted and asked to come in. Harassed mothers were glad of a sympathetic ear into which they could pour their troubles. Old people living alone looked forward each week to the visit from the young ladies. Edel was a good listener and never seemed to be in a hurry. Even when she said nothing, her presence brought comfort and reassurance.

A typical example of her gift for bringing peace was shown in the case of Miss Young, who suffered from a form of paranoia. She believed that her neighbours across the landing were persecuting her, knocking at her door and trying to destroy her peace of mind. Edel was the only one who could calm her and she visited her regularly. She often had to spend two or three hours at a time listening to her troubles before the poor woman would let her go.

At the same time, it is no cliché to say that she received as much as she gave. She saw people enduring hardship without complaint, accepting suffering as the will of God. Her own troubles seemed slight by comparison. She discovered depths of spirituality where she least expected it. One of those she visited was a namesake of hers, Mrs Quinn, a convert to Catholicism and an avid reader. Mrs Quinn had a special love for the writings of St John of the Cross. She and Edel talked about prayer and the life of the spirit and exchanged their favourite books.

At the weekly meeting Edel reported on her work simply and factually, with no attempt to draw attention to herself. Yet she could not help drawing the attention of others, among them a new member named Mary Walls who was later to become a close friend of hers. She has left us a sharply observed account of her first impressions of Edel.

> The first thing that struck me was the unusual brightness of her eyes and the wonderful charm of her smile. She was always well dressed, with perfect taste and according to the fashion. She was among the moderns of her time, but was not ultra-modern; she avoided such things as lip-stick. Her clothes were in keeping with rules of modesty, though without priggishness.
>
> She had a most attractive personality. Her general attitude and manner gave an impression of great friendliness. Her greeting on the occasion of a chance meeting was always brimming over with warmth. She simply swept you off your feet, such was the whole-heartedness of her handshake and of her cheery greeting. 'Hello, how are you?' or 'What a pleasant surprise!'
>
> One sensed about her a consciousness of living in the divine presence. She did not talk about it, but her personality radiated an

atmosphere of recollection. Yet she was the soul of gaiety, of cheerfulness. That was one of the most extraordinary aspects of her whole conduct: quite naturally and seemingly with perfect ease she combined a deep interior life with all the assets of social success – youth, charm, smartness, love of fun and innocent merriment, a keen sense of humour, a bright intelligence, a talent for music and ability at sports such as tennis, dancing and golf, all of which she loved but gave up to devote herself more fully to the Legion apostolate.

Others also noticed how the Legion was beginning to take over more and more of Edel's life. The Legion rule stipulated that each member should spend two hours a week on apostolic work in addition to the time at the meeting. Edel fulfilled this obligation by her weekly visitation. But as her relationship developed with the people she visited, she found herself returning on other evenings and on Sunday afternoons. She became involved in other work as well, especially in visiting patients in the Mater Misericordiae Hospital, where her sympathy and cheerfulness made her many friends. She was always willing to help other Praesidia in running special events and projects and she became more and more widely known as someone who could be called on at any time.

It was not long before her name reached the ears of the founder of the Legion himself. Frank Duff, born in Dublin in 1889, was a civil servant by profession. As a young man he joined the Society of St Vincent de Paul but gradually came to feel the need for another group to complement the work of the society. He had in mind a group which would concentrate on spiritual rather than material aid and which would admit women to membership. In 1921 he achieved his aim and set up the first meeting of the Association of Our Lady of Mercy, soon to be renamed the Legion of Mary.

Frank Duff had a remarkable gift for organisation and part of it was his ability to to spot promising new talent. The Legion was expanding rapidly. By 1927 there were thirteen Praesidia in Dublin and in that same year the first one outside Dublin was established in

Waterford. The following year the Legion appeared in Scotland and by 1930 a start had been made in France, India and the United States. There was urgent need of able and dedicated members who would take on positions of leadership in the growing movement.

The reports he was hearing about Edel Quinn were promising. He decided to see for himself. He did not want to set up a formal meeting which might alarm her so he contrived to meet her casually. They met, spoke together, and formed their first impressions of one another.

Edel saw before her a man in his early forties, short in stature, slight in build. He had a bright eye which missed nothing and a pleasant smile. His manner was friendly and informal. He spoke slowly and softly and listened attentively, sometimes cupping his hand behind his ear, a sign of his growing deafness. There was nothing about him that would inspire awe, yet there was a kind of aura that spoke of immense reserves of energy and strength. Behind his placid exterior was a will and a determination that matched her own.

He has described his first impressions of her. 'She was terribly impressive,' he said, 'very girlish indeed but a very refreshing experience.' He found everything about her attractive, her smile, her humour, her beauty. 'That's a lovely girl,' he said to himself, 'a lovely girl.' He filed her face and name in his remarkable memory as someone who would have much to contribute to the Legion in years to come.

Some time later he invited her to his house for tea. His house, which doubled as the Legion headquarters, was the former residence of the master of the North Dublin Workhouse. The workhouse had been handed over to the Legion by the government and turned into two hostels for the homeless, the Morning Star Hostel for men and the Regina Coeli Hostel for women and children. The master's house was a modest red-brick building and Frank lived here with his widowed mother, his brother and sisters.

The more he saw of Edel, the more his respect for her grew. A shrewd judge of others, he saw remarkable qualities of head and heart in this young girl. He wrote:

> Her charm of manner was supreme but it went far deeper than the
> surface. There was nothing of the artificial in her. She attracted
> people very strongly. In trying to analyse this fact, one is thrown
> back on that suggestion which Chesterton makes about St Francis
> of Assisi: that the secret of the Saint's power lay in the conviction
> which people gained that he was really interested in each one of
> them. I would say that anyone who spoke with Edel Quinn ended
> up with that same idea. As a consequence they loved her and
> wanted to do what she asked of them.

He himself felt that attraction very strongly. It was not a purely
spiritual attraction. In an interview recorded forty years later, he said
he had been drawn to her as a man is drawn to a beautiful and attractive woman. 'I'd say that I was terribly impressed by her as a girl. Of
course, as I have always stated, I always reckon she could have had
any man she wanted.' He recalled again her charm, her smile, her
playfulness, her extraordinary beauty. 'There is a far higher form of
beauty than the film-star beauty that causes men to look round after
girls as they pass in the street. I've always said that Our Lady must
have been indescribably beautiful but I don't think that men would
look round after her in the street.' That was the kind of beauty he
saw in Edel.

'I do not know,' he went on, 'what way my thoughts would have
operated in regard to Edel Quinn if I had been up to marriage. I
never was. I made up my mind as a very very young man I was
never going to get married and in that course I never wavered for a
second. But I have to admit that I was certainly impressed by Edel
Quinn as a woman.' When asked if he thought that she was attracted
towards him he replied, 'I would believe that if any sort of a chance
existed, Edel's affections could have been fixed on me. I would believe that, I would believe that.'

No such chance existed. Frank had embraced a life of celibacy by
a conscious resolution. Edel had similarly bound herself by her

commitment to the life of a Poor Clare sister. Each of them had, in Newman's phrase, 'a high severe idea of the intrinsic excellence of virginity.' Neither of them was the kind to put a hand to the plough and then turn back. Their relationship was that of St Francis and St Clare, all the more fruitful in the spirit because it transcended the flesh.

It was not long before an opportunity arose of using Edel's gifts. Colette Gill, president of the Praesidium of Our Lady Refuge of Sinners, offered her resignation. Frank Duff asked Edel if she was willing to take the position of president in her place. It was one of the most difficult Praesidia in the Legion, the Praesidium that worked with the prostitutes of the city. She was not yet twenty-five and had led a sheltered middle-class life. She seemed a strange choice for the job. But Frank knew what he was doing and spoke to her very persuasively.

'There was a great simplicity about her,' he recalled, 'and if you told her that you thought she was the person for it, she would assent to that and she'd probably assent no matter what its gravity was.' She didn't ask for time to reflect or pray about her decision. She accepted on the spot.

FIVE

Refuge of Sinners

Edel's initiation into her new job proved to be something of an ordeal. The Praesidium of Our Lady Refuge of Sinners met in Myra House, where the Legion had been founded in 1921. The meeting at which she presided for the first time followed the invariable format of Legion meetings. After the opening prayers came the reading and signing of the minutes and the short spiritual reading. Then the members began to give their reports.

Almost from the beginning the Legion had worked among prostitutes. One of their earliest campaigns led to the closing down of the brothels in the area around Montgomery Street, the Nighttown of Joyce's *Ulysses*. But the problem was far from solved. There were still many prostitutes operating in other parts of the city. Even those who had been persuaded to give up prostitution were always liable to relapse because they had no other means of livelihood and no other place to live. For this reason, the Legion had opened a house in Harcourt St, the Sancta Maria Hostel, where street-girls could be housed and given a chance to rehabilitate themselves. Much of the work of the Praesidium of Our Lady Refuge of Sinners centred around the Sancta Maria Hostel and its unpredictable residents.

As the meeting went on, Edel became more and more conscious of the responsibility she was undertaking and the kind of work she was facing. That in itself could have been a reason for some misgivings. But there was a much stronger reason. Edel, with her sensitivity to others, must have been aware that she was being scrutinised and judged and that the judgement was far from favourable. Nothing was said, everyone was kind and courteous, but the reality was there. She had been tried and found wanting.

The meeting ended, the spiritual director gave the blessing, Edel left for home. The others remained on. Then the real meeting began. The feeling of indignation was universal. The work they did was exceptionally difficult and delicate. They had specifically asked Head-quarters for a new president with the weight and experience to cope with the demands. Instead they had been sent a mere slip of a girl, no doubt a pious and innocent girl, but with none of the wisdom and maturity that were needed. 'A child has been sent to lead us,' they said. For the sake of the Praesidium, for the sake of the Hostel, for the sake of the Legion, she must be replaced by someone less patently inadequate.

They decided to make a protest to Headquarters. The spiritual director, Father Dempsey, was appointed spokesman. He crossed the city to Brother Duff's house and put the case before him. Frank heard him out and then put his side of the case. He spoke of Edel's qualities as he had come to know and appreciate them. He promised that she would prove a more than worthy successor to Sister Gill. More to the point, he made it crystal clear that his mind was made up and he had absolutely no intention of changing it. Father Dempsey returned to the malcontents with the bad news. 'I cut no ice,' he said.

It proved to be a storm in a teacup. Faced with the inevitable, the members accepted their new president. It took only a very short while before they realised what a treasure they had been given. Her mild and unassuming manner was deceptive. She ran the meetings smoothly and competently. She organised the work efficiently. She inspired the members to new vigour and commitment. She asked them to do nothing that she was not ready to do herself.

Edel had met prostitutes now and then while doing visitation for her previous Praesidium. At that time it had been a problem that she occasionally encountered. Now it was one in which she was totally immersed. The work took various forms. Much of her time was spent in making contact with the girls, talking to them on the street or visiting them in the miserable lodging houses where they lived, often in conditions of extreme squalor. Harassed by police, bullied by pimps, exploited by madams, fleeced by landlords, despised by the men who used them, their life was a wretched one. It was rarely that they saw a kind face or heard a kind word.

Many of them found their hearts touched by this pretty young girl who spoke so gently and listened so sympathetically. They were almost all Catholics, with a faith that somehow survived the conditions of their daily life. They wore a medal or a cross, they treasured somewhere a crucifix or a rosary or a statue of Our Lady, they still remembered how to say the Hail Mary and make the sign of the cross. When she asked them to come away for a day's retreat or a weekend or to visit the Sancta Maria Hostel, they were at least prepared to listen. She was saying nothing that they hadn't heard before. Yet when she said it, it sounded different. She made it seem possible to hope again.

The Sancta Maria Hostel offered a half-way house for those who were trying to change their way of life. It enabled them to get away for a while from their old environment. It provided them with food and shelter while they tried to make the transition to a regular job and a normal life.

It was a place of hope but also a place of tension. The street-girls who came to live there did not acquire stability and self-control overnight. They had years of frustration and aggression to work off. Some of them were mentally unbalanced, some were dependent on drugs, many were addicted to alcohol. There were frequent quarrels, verbal attacks and physical assaults. There were constant threats to leave and return to the streets, threats which could all too easily be carried out.

If Edel had any fantasies about being surrounded by grateful reformed Magdalens, they were soon shattered by the dirty, drunken, foul-mouthed reality. The early days were hard. One of her Legion friends remembered finding Edel in tears after a particularly unpleasant scene; it was the only time she ever saw Edel crying. But she soon learned to cope. Another friend related how one night the girls turned against the Legionaries, abusing them scurrilously and at length. After it all died down, she saw Edel having a friendly chat with one of her attackers as if nothing had happened. They were talking about Cork.

In order to prevent incidents of this kind, Edel tried to provide constant activities and diversions for the girls. The skills she had developed while working with the Loreto club proved very useful. At weekends she often arranged outings. On one occasion she said she was going to see some friends in Loreto Abbey, Rathfarnham, and asked if anyone would like to come with her. The arrival of the group from Sancta Maria at the Abbey, one of Ireland's most select boarding schools, must have provided an interesting confrontation.

In the evenings she played the piano and taught them to dance. She organised charades and improvised dramas. 'Mary, you'll be the mother. Kitty, you're the father. The rest of you are the children. Now, listen, this is what it's about.' She described the story-line for them, assigning roles suited to the talents of the different girls and making sure that nobody was left out. One would be given a song to sing, another would be asked to dance. She became adept at spinning out the proceedings and making them last until it was time for bed. Then, some time about midnight, she would head off for the train to Seapoint and home.

As the months passed, she spent more and more of her time in the Hostel. Most of her evenings and much of her weekends were taken up with Legion work. Even her lunch break was often sacrificed for the cause. She had little time for any kind of recreation. There was scarcely any tennis and even less dancing. Her family hardly saw her and began to worry about her. Her Legion colleagues were equally concerned. One of them, Jo McCrossan, described a typical incident.

One time Edel and I were going along Abbey Street. It was about 8 p.m. and we were intending to spend the evening together, at the pictures or somewhere like that. Edel noticed a girl some distance away and with a quick word of explanation she abandoned me in Abbey Street to follow the girl and persuade her to go to Sancta Maria. I asked her afterwards what time it was when she succeeded in her plan and she told me it must have been round about midnight. I remember this because I was amazed at the way she went off to follow the girl and kept after her until midnight. She apologised to me, knowing well that I wouldn't take any offence.

People began to notice that she was looking tired. Her colour was poor and she was coughing a lot. She seemed to be losing weight. She was certainly working too hard and probably not eating enough. No-one knew exactly what she ate or when she ate it.

She didn't eat at home: she left each morning before seven on her way to Mass and didn't get back until after midnight. Her sister, Leslie, worked with her at Chagny Tiles and Mrs Quinn would tell her to be sure and bring Edel home for lunch, but when the time came Edel would make some excuse and Leslie would come home alone. When challenged by her mother, Edel would laugh it off. 'I had a cup of tea in the Hostel,' she would say. The fact remained that the only square meal her family ever saw her eat was the Sunday lunch.

Others noticed the same thing. When she visited Frank Duff for tea, she took neither milk nor sugar. 'I argued with her about that because she gave me the impression of fragility,' he said. 'She assured me that was the way she liked it and that it wasn't out of penance that she was doing it.' It was the same story when she visited Robert's Café with an old friend from Upton. She was content with a cup of black tea and declined to have a cake or bun. 'I had my lunch,' she said.

Someone asked Nancy Hogg, her former president, to have a word with her. Nancy met her at the funeral of a deceased Legionary in Whitefriar Street Church. It was a golden opportunity. Nancy asked her a few pointed questions about her current life-style. Was she at the Hostel last night? What time did she leave for home? Did she not think she was worrying her family?

'My family?' said Edel cheerfully. 'Oh, they've given me up as a bad job.'

'If you're not careful,' said Nancy, 'we'll be having Mass said for another dead Legionary.'

'That would be fine,' said Edel and laughed. The laughing was soon to stop. It is difficult at this distance in time to determine how far Edel was undermining her health by her sparse diet. All the witnesses agree that she seemed to eat very little during this period, though she concealed the fact to the best of her ability. When invited to a formal meal, she would eat normally and appear to enjoy her food. But when left on her own, the suspicion was that she took barely enough to sustain life.

The thought must occur to any modern reader that she could have been suffering from anorexia nervosa. The disease was less known in the 1930s than it is today but it certainly existed. Some aspects of Edel's behaviour would support such a diagnosis. The disease occurs most often in young women. Its main symptom is an extreme reluctance to eat, resulting first in loss of weight and eventually in the collapse of the whole system. It is rooted in psychological problems, including the sufferer's rejection of her own sexuality. She becomes adept at concealing the fact that she is not eating and manages to persuade others that she has already eaten or is about to eat somewhere else. It is not until her physical deterioration has become very noticeable that her family and friends become aware of what is happening.

All these symptoms seem to be present in Edel's case. Yet there are reasons for not accepting this diagnosis. The disease usually shows itself first in the middle to late teens. Edel's own teen-age years were notably happy and healthy. The disease is neurotic in origin. No-one who knew Edel ever saw anything neurotic about her. The disease is generally linked with the sufferer's fear that she has lost control of her life as a result of being dominated by her parents. Edel's relations with her parents were always close and affectionate. Far from being dominated by them, she herself was the dominant person in the home. It is safest to accept the opinion of those who knew her best at the time. They believed that she restricted her food quite simply and solely for religious motives. The practice of fasting was recommended by the spiritual writers she read and the preachers she heard, following the words and example of Jesus himself. The law of the Church at the time called for abstinence from meat on all Fridays. In addition, those over twenty-one were bound to observe a fast during the forty days of Lent and some other days of the year which permitted only one full meal each day. Such a fast was enough for most people but not for Edel. Her ardent and generous spirit led her to go beyond the bounds of law and beyond the bounds of prudence. She had no idea that her lungs were already infected by tuberculosis and that she had need of more food than the average person, not less.

Early in 1932 her brother Ralph celebrated his twenty-first birthday. A birthday dance was organised to mark the event. It was the night of Edel's Praesidium meeting and she was faced with a conflict of loyalties. She solved it in typical fashion by presiding at the meeting in her evening dress and then going straight on to the party. The financial situation of the family had improved greatly. There were now three salaries coming into 22 Trafalgar Terrace in addition to her own. Her father was still working in the bank and Leslie in the Chagny Tile Company. Ralph had succeeded in passing his examinations and was now employed like his father in the National Bank. There was no longer the same need for her own contribution. She began to make her plans for entering the convent.

Her original intention had been to join the community of Poor Clares on Simmonscourt Road in Dublin. She visited the convent on a number of occasions and was greatly attracted by their spirituality and way of life. Unlike the sisters in the various schools she had attended, the Poor Clares were a contemplative order. A large part of their day was devoted to prayer and contemplation. The different hours of the Divine Office were recited aloud by the whole community at the appropriate times each day. There was also time set aside for private prayer and spiritual reading. The food was simple, the accommodation was spartan. They followed the pattern of St Francis, the poor man of Assisi, and tried to let nothing material come between them and God.

Edel sometimes brought her sister Leslie with her to the convent. Like every visitor, Leslie was struck by the door which seemed to open without the help of human hands and the parlour where disembodied voices came from behind a grille in one of the walls. On one occasion the nuns opened the grille and she saw them for the only time in their brown Franciscan habits.

It was on this visit that the question of Belfast was decided. The community were as impressed with Edel as she was with them, and were happy to welcome her into their company. But there was another Poor Clare convent in Ireland which was going through a difficult time. It was in Belfast, a city where Catholics were a minority subjected to constant discrimination and occasional violence. The nuns there were finding it hard to attract vocations. Would Edel consider going to Belfast instead of Simmonscourt Road?

It meant a sacrifice for the Dublin community, who would be losing a valuable addition to their number. It meant an even greater sacrifice for Edel. Simmonscourt Road was only a short tram-ride from Monkstown. Belfast was a hundred miles away, in an area which most southern Catholics regarded with fear and distrust. Visits from her family would be few and far between. Characteristically, Edel ignored such considerations. Yes, she said, she would be happy to go to Belfast.

She travelled to Belfast and spent a day there in the convent. The arrangements were made. The date was decided. On the 25 March 1932 she was to enter the Convent of the Poor Clares. It was the Feast of the Annunciation, the day when Mary was asked to become the mother of God and answered Yes.

It was only now, in January 1932, that Edel began to tell her friends of her decision. The news spread quickly. Mary Walls met her on a Sunday morning in St Stephen's Green. 'In response to her usual breezy greeting, I reproached her for not having given me the news, which I had just learned elsewhere, of her approaching entry to a convent. She apologised, saying that she wanted to be certain of her entry before letting the word get around.'

Reactions were mixed. Many congratulated her, sharing in her obvious happiness. Vocations to the religious life were by no means uncommon among her friends, especially her Legionary friends. Mary Walls herself became a Carthusian not long afterwards. But there was also genuine sadness at losing someone who was so good a friend and so valued a colleague. The Praesidium of Our Lady Refuge of Sinners, which had once resisted her appointment as President, was devastated. Under her leadership it had grown in numbers and enthusiasm. Where would they find a replacement?

There was similar devastation in the Children of Mary Club in North Great George's St, which she still managed to attend in the midst of all her other activities. Jo McCrossan, another of the helpers in the club, heard the news and told her how sorry she was to see her go. A few nights later, Edel had some more news for her.

One evening while we were leaving the Club, she told me with a smile that my wish for her not to go away had been granted. She had had a haemorrhage. She said it with a smile as if it was a joke. I was amazed how calmly she took it. She gave me the impression that she took everything that happened to her as the will of God. She accepted it in a way that I could never have done.

This second item of news went around even more quickly than the first. In those days when tuberculosis was so common and so feared among young adults, everyone knew what the word haemorrhage implied. A flow of blood from the mouth was a sign that the lungs had been seriously infected by the disease. In many cases it was a sentence of death.

Edel never told her friends about the circumstances of this first haemorrhage or her reaction to it. Some clue to her feelings might be found in a book which was constantly in her hands, *The Story of a Soul* by St Thérèse of Lisieux. Edel would have been familiar with the passage where the saint undergoes the same traumatic experience in the early hours of Good Friday 1896. In the version read by Edel it goes as follows:

I could not obtain permission to remain watching at the Altar of Repose throughout the Thursday night, and I returned to our cell at midnight. Scarcely was my head laid on the pillow when I felt a hot stream rise to my lips. I thought I was going to die, and my heart nearly broke with joy. But as I had already put out our lamp, I mortified my curiosity until the morning and slept in peace. At five o'clock, when it was time to get up, I remembered at once that I had some good news to learn, and going to the window I found, as I had expected, that our handkerchief was soaked with blood. Dearest Mother, what hope was mine! I was firmly convinced that on this anniversary of His Death, my Beloved had allowed me to hear His first call, like a sweet, distant murmur, heralding His joyful approach.

The resemblance between Thérèse and Edel had been commented on by others. Now they had a further link in common. The saint's example must have helped Edel to accept the haemorrhage with that calm and serenity that astonished all her friends.

She went to the local doctor for an examination. Dr Scribrier did not mince his words. She was suffering from tuberculosis of the lungs and the disease was far advanced. She must go to a sanatorium as soon as possible and stay there until she was cured. It was likely to take a very long time.

SIX

The Sanatorium

On 5 February 1932 Edel was admitted as a patient to Newcastle sanatorium, one of a ring of sanatoriums that circled Dublin city in those days. It was built in the foothills of the Wicklow Mountains, about twenty-five miles from the city and just two miles from the sea.

The drugs that were to revolutionise the treatment of tuberculosis had not yet been discovered. There was no known cure. All that a sanatorium could do was provide fresh air, good food and a restful stress-free environment. It was hoped that the body's own natural powers of recovery would do the rest.

The atmosphere of a sanatorium was quite unlike that of an ordinary hospital. Most of the patients were young, between the late teens and the early thirties. It was quite usual for them to stay there for six months or a year. If the disease had not advanced too far, they did not have to stay in bed. They could wander around the wards and walk in the grounds. There was plenty of time for friendships to develop and in a mixed sanatorium like Newcastle these could easily develop into romances. In some ways it resembled a slow motion holiday camp.

In other ways it resembled a prison. Discipline was strict. Patients could not leave the grounds without permission. They had to turn up faithfully and punctually in the dining-room for all meals. Twice a day, at noon and 4 p.m., they attended a roll-call and answered 'Present' when their names were called out, after which they went to their beds for a compulsory rest period. Occasional entertainments and visits from friends broke the monotony, but most days were long and empty and idle. There was plenty of time for them to brood over their uncertain future.

Edel must have had her dark days and her sleepless nights like everyone else, but she showed no sign of it. Patients and visitors alike found her always cheerful. She was clearly helped by her deep faith and her total resignation to the will of God. Her concern for the troubles of others helped her to forget her own.

The sanatorium had a number of rooms for private patients. Edel could not afford to pay for this luxury and was registered as a public patient. Her insurance covered the cost of a public ward, which she shared with four or five others, and provided her with a weekly spending allowance of twelve shillings and sixpence. Her ward-mates were not always pleasant company and their language could leave a good deal to be desired, but she did not complain. She made many friends among the patients and recruited a good number of them to become auxiliary members of the Legion and help the work by their daily prayers.

One of her fellow-patients was Mrs Josephine Brady. She was only seventeen when she arrived in Newcastle, two months after Edel.

> I was very young and very sick and I found myself with about fifty or sixty girls waiting to go to breakfast. It was my first morning there. No-one bothered about me and I was feeling lonely and miserable when this girl came over to me. She was smiling and gentle and kind and she took me by the arm. She said she would show me where to go and look after me. She helped me to walk the hundred yards to the dining-room and she put me sitting down with my back to the men. I think it was out of consideration for me.
>
> She was very kind also to another Protestant girl, an orphan, who was about ten years old and had only one arm. She took special care of Vicky. She used to cut up her meat into little pieces and help her at meals. If Edel went out to tea, which was allowed once a month or so, she sometimes took Vicky with her. Vicky used to call her 'my Mammy.' She died.

All day long Edel was at the beck and call of others. Some of the patients were poorly educated. Edel would read and write letters for them. On Mondays and Fridays a dance was organised for the patients. Edel was always there to play the piano. 'One evening someone else took her place,' Mrs Brady recalled, 'and when Edel was free a man asked her to dance. I remember being surprised that she wanted to dance. She really danced very well and she was completely at ease with men.'

Another fellow-patient was Winnie Leavy who became a good friend of Edel's and remained so until the end of her life. She too noticed how attentive she was to the needs of others. The staff as well as the patients came to rely on her. One night a young nurse asked her to come to someone who was close to death. Winnie remembered her running across the concrete floor of the open verandah, barefoot and in a light dressing gown, to help with the dying patient. Even the matron, before whom the whole sanatorium trembled, was won over by her. She declared afterwards that Edel was the nicest patient they had ever had.

She never complained about her illness or about any of the discomforts and inconveniences of hospital life. She admitted to only two things that she found painful, both of them connected with her religion. One was a small incident that happened when she was going to confession. She noticed the priest drawing away from her as if he was afraid of contagion. It was only a small thing but it hurt.

The other was more important. Newcastle was a Protestant sanatorium. There was no chapel and no Blessed Sacrament. Mass was said for the patients on Sundays and holy days only. All her life she had been accustomed to daily Mass and Holy Communion and she found the deprivation hard to bear. She told Winnie she would never again go to any place where there was no daily Mass.

In the absence of the Church's liturgy, she made her own routine. It was noticed that she spent a long time in private prayer every morning. Each day she said the Little Office of Our Lady. She spent a good deal of time in spiritual reading. She used to lead the patients in her ward in the recitation of the Rosary. More controversially, she still performed acts of penance. She never ate sweets or fruit between meals. At dinner she gave her dessert to someone else. She did the same with the glass of milk that was given to her every morning and night. It may be that she made up for these by eating heartily of the plainer foods. Still it was imprudent, to say the least.

The distance from Dublin made it hard for people to visit her. Someone from the family came most weekends. Her friends from the Legion came down regularly, often in groups of three or four. They found her always cheerful and smiling, determined to let none of the pain show through. She stonewalled all their questions. When they inquired about her health, it was 'all right'. When they asked about life in the sanatorium, it was 'very funny'. The two phrases were constantly on her lips. It was quite evident to them that everything was not all right. The weeks turned into months and they could still see no improvement in her condition. The ward where she had her bed was an open verandah. There was a roof to keep off most of the rain, but no front wall to keep out the bitter winter winds. Strange though it may seem, this was normal in sanatoriums of the period. Fresh air was one of the main ingredients in the treatment of tuberculosis sufferers, and the more air they got and the fresher it was, the sooner they were expected to recover. Edel's visitors sat miserably beside her, shivering in their hats and coats and furs and gloves, and saw her own face and hands blue with the cold. The cure seemed worse than the disease.

One of her regular visitors was Mary Walls. A year older than Edel, she nonetheless looked up to her as someone who was her spiritual superior. She usually went alone, so that they could talk freely together. Mary was in search of a spiritual director and she asked Edel if she would take on the responsibility. Edel declined and admitted that she had the same problem. They agreed that they would both pray for a spiritual director who would meet their needs.

As time went on, the bond between the two grew stronger. Eventually Mary was to become her closest friend. The more she came to know Edel, the more she wondered at her depth and perception. Edel remained uncommunicative about her own interior life, but she spoke about the things of the spirit with remarkable sureness and insight, drawing on a wide reading of theology and spirituality.

She was so clearly at home discussing the deep mysteries of the Faith, that I felt sure she had a certain experimental knowledge of them. So, although I cannot now remember her exact words in these discussions, I do recall their subject matter.

She spoke most frequently about the indwelling of the Blessed Trinity in the soul, having perhapss been led to that by the teaching and preaching of the Carmelite Father who had previously been her confessor. He had particularly recommended some little books which we both read and reread with great profit, *One with Jesus* by De Jaegher and *From Holy Communion to the Blessed Trinity* by Bernadot, but also the works of Père Plus: *God within Us*, *In Christ Jesus* and *Christ in his Brethren*.

Then we found other books of equal interest: the works of Dom Marmion and St John of the Cross; and the *True Devotion* and the *Secret of Mary* of St Louis Marie de Montfort. These of course were 'daily bread' for Legionaries. The *Life* and other writings of the Little Flower were great favourites. In fact, the book entitled *L'Esprit de Ste Thérèse* became one of Edel's most cherished possession. She had it in French and evidently applied

Edel's friend, Mary Walls (aged 23), who later entered the Carthusian Monastery at Giaveno in northern Italy, as Sister Mary Celestine.

herself to living constantly according to its teaching.

Other favourite authors of hers were Juliana of Norwich, Elizabeth Leseur, Sr Elizabeth of the Trinity and *Consummata*. She also read works of Vonier, and Tanquerey's *A Treatise of the Spiritual Life* and many others of which I cannot give a complete list, not to mention the New Testament and *The Imitation of Christ* which were the most frequently read of all. I tried to make her read *The Interior Castle* of St Teresa, but she refused to go beyond the first four chapters, saying that she considered it a waste of time to read about extraordinary graces of which she had no personal experience.

Spring passed into summer, summer into autumn. She had now spent the better part of a year in the sanatorium. Many of those who came after her left before her, given a clean bill of health after a stay of six months or less. Her own condition showed no sign of improving. The doctors looked at her x-rays and shook their heads.

She began to grow impatient. It seemed to her that she was wasting time staying in Newcastle, time that could be better used elsewhere. And she was worried about her family. 'I'll have to leave here and go back to work,' she told a Legion friend, Muriel Wailes. 'My parents can't stand the expense of keeping me here any longer.' It may be that her insurance cover had expired or that there were other expenses to be borne. In any event, some time before Christmas 1932 she decided to leave.

One of her Legion friends was Dr John Keane, a scientist and university professor and the possessor of a motor car. He drove down one Sunday to see Edel and was surprised when she told him she was leaving the sanatorium and asked him to drive her home. When he agreed, she collected her belongings, got into the car and was driven back to Dublin. He brought her all the way to Trafalgar Terrace, where she was welcomed by her delighted but astonished family.

It has been suggested that she left Newcastle without the approval of her medical advisers and that she acted in a hasty and imprudent manner. There is no direct evidence to prove or disprove this. But it would be quite uncharacteristic of Edel to go without being properly discharged. She was noted in the sanatorium for her exact observance of all the rules. She was always punctual for meals and roll-calls, she kept strictly to the areas open to public patients, she made a point of returning from walks in the grounds at the appointed time. It was in her character to act swiftly once she had made her decision. It was not in her character to act without proper consideration for those in authority.

She never lost contact with the friends she had made in the sanatorium. One of her companions in the ward had been a girl called Maureen Dooley, who was transferred to a Dublin nursing home, The Cedars. Edel went to see her when she got back to Dublin and found her very weak. A couple of days later, Maureen died. Edel wrote a letter of sympathy to her mother which reveals something of her own feelings towards her illness.

> She was so contented to die, and so resigned, when it was God's will, and she liked the Cedars, as she was able to receive Holy Communion a few times a week, so different to Newcastle.
>
> I am sure her prayers will help you to feel more resigned. I know that she is happier now, and honestly as one who has had the same complaint, I would not mind changing places with her. It is really a relief to be at peace, after being just an invalid even for a year, though one good thing about it is, one has no pain at all during all the illness, which is something to be thankful for.

Edel continued to keep in touch with the family, as she kept in touch with all her friends. A letter written to Maureen's sister in April 1933 describes the very limited progress she was making.

> I am sure you wonder that I have not written before, but since Christmas my arrangements have been altering, dependent on consecutive doses of flu and periods of recovery! The last recovery period I spent my time arranging to get a light job abroad, and when I had it all settled got the last dose which left me where I

started, so that now I am under a specialist in town and he is to try some new serum – purely experimental – after Easter, and I believe it will be the end of summer before it will be over. I don't know what the actual effects are but it is like vaccination, I believe, it may be rather hectic! However, God's will be done.

At her mother's insistence, she continued to see various specialists and sample various remedies. In August she was still experimenting or being experimented upon, as we know from a letter she wrote to Pierre Landrin. He had been constantly on the move, living in England, America, Spain and Algeria. Now he wrote from Germany telling her of the latest so-called cure. Her reply is the last in the series of letters to him.

I was very interested to hear of the 'nature cure'. The damp ground and compresses of cold water gave me cold shivers, though! One or two 'specialists' here are great advocates of nature cure, in the line of rest, wholesome food and exercise, an out-of-door life. A lot depends on the grip of disease on one in this.

I enclose a leaflet giving particulars of 'Stevens' cure; whether one has to take a lot of it with a pinch of salt or not is hard to know. Certainly the medicine has a definite effect with the cough and breathing; in my case the former has disappeared and the latter is much easier. I have a fair amount of literature from him concerning it; in any event one doctor in Switzerland who has tried it, has had 202 cures in five years, supposed to be all the cases he tried it on in that period.

However, on the strength of it, I am back at work again. Of course, the Doc. says there is now a cavity on top of left lung but the right is still untouched. However, as I felt able, I looked for a job, advertised, I got into Callow's of Westland Row, motor people, first premises after Church and Christian Brothers' School, Westland Row. They are an old established firm, going back to coach building days; they have also a good deal of property in Dublin and outside.

Despite their cheerful tone, these letters give a sad glimpse into the world of the tuberculosis sufferer in the nineteen-thirties. It was a world she shared with many others, a world of alternating hope and despair, a world of quack medicines and miracle cures, a world of worrying about symptoms and clutching at straws. Perhaps she had not coughed on the day she wrote the letter, perhaps her breathing was easier, whatever that may mean. The brutal fact remained that she was not cured, and she knew it.

Her letter to Pierre went on to give further details about her life-style in general and her job in Callow's in particular.

They are a decent crowd to work with, two brothers are partners, they have about thirty people employed, there are two of us in the office. I have been there since July 1st. All during the heat wave they kept us well supplied with ice cream!! There is plenty of work to be done; of course, nearly every night I go to bed at 9 p.m. which is respectable. Of course, they too have been hit by Dev's tariffs. They build motor bodies; they also now have made one or two caravans – the latter might appeal to you.

The job at Callow's was not as idyllic as she made it out to be. The office where she worked was a partitioned-off section of the body-shop, lit only by electric light. Her friends noticed that the air which she breathed was full of paint fumes and metallic dust, neither of them helpful to her damaged lungs. When her doctor heard about the conditions she was working in, he warned her of the danger. She treated the warning as a huge joke.

Gradually her life returned to normal. She make good resolutions about eating meals regularly and going to bed early and her family made sure that she kept them, at least for a time. She showed no signs of worrying about her own condition, but she was very concerned about the danger to the health of her sisters and brother, especially Leslie, with whom she shared a bedroom. She told them she would have to sleep alone in future, as she could not expose them to the risk of contracting the disease from her.

The flat was small and had no spare bedrooms. Either they would have to move house, or Edel would have to leave and find a bedsitter for herself. The family found both solutions equally unacceptable. But Edel was absolutely firm on the point. Careless about her own health, she was scrupulously careful about the health of the others. When it became clear that she was serious about leaving home, her parents yielded. They were fortunate to find a suitable house a short distance away at no. 42 Monkstown Road and they moved there at once. It was to be Edel's home for the remainder of her life in Ireland.

The Legion of Mary still beckoned. Her mother was understandably opposed to the idea that she would resume her work for the prostitutes of the city. Even Edel herself was forced to admit that she lacked the health and stamina for all the late nights and stressful confrontations involved. She reached a compromise with her mother and found a Praesidium that enabled her to resume her Legion links without unduly taxing her strength.

The Regina Coeli Praesidium met in Temple Hill Children's Hospital, a few minutes' walk from her home. The President was her old friend Mona McCarthy, who could be guaranteed to keep a watchful eye on her. Edel herself was appointed to the not very onerous position of Vice-President. The other members were student nurses in the hospital, which was under the care of the Sisters of Charity of St Vincent de Paul. No outside visitation was involved and Edel's duties consisted mainly in attending the weekly meeting. On most evenings she could come home from work, eat a normal evening meal with the rest of the family and then go to bed. Even her mother had to admit that she seemed to be behaving quite sensibly.

One stabilising factor in her life was her new spiritual director. Shortly after her return from the sanatorium, her friend Mary Walls told her about a young priest she had met, Father Dermot Boylan, who impressed her greatly by his discernment and spirituality. She felt that he was the director that both of them had been seeking. Edel met him and was equally impressed. They both adopted him as their regular confessor. Every Saturday afternoon they went to confession to him, and they often spent the rest of the evening together in one or other of their homes or in some quiet spot near the sea.

Edel did not tell her friend very much about what was said to her in the secrecy of the confessional. Still Mary had the definite impression that it was Father Boylan's influence that led her to adopt a less penitential life-style. It was out of obedience to him that she ate the food her mother served her, including meat, and increased her time of rest by making her meditation in bed in the mornings and going to a later Mass. She consulted him about every aspect of her life and followed his guidance without question, as Mary came to realise.

It often happened that, while we were walking along together after confession, our confessor passed us by on his bicycle, saluting us in passing. One day, as this happened, I said to Edel, 'I wonder what he thinks of our being so often together?' Whereupon Edel replied: 'Oh, it is all right; he approves of our friendship. I asked him.' That reassured me, but also surprised me, for it had never occurred to me to ask his approval. It gave me an insight into the delicacy of Edel's conscience.

She confided in Mary more than in any of her other friends. She admitted to her that she still had haemorrhages from the lungs from time to time. When this happened, she took a day off work and nothing more. From time to time, her conversation would be interrupted by terrible bouts of coughing. As soon as the fit had subsided, she would continue as if nothing had happened. Any inquiries about her health were parried and the subject was skilfully changed. She was determined to live as full and normal a life as possible. She had obeyed the doctors for more than a year and they had failed. She would now use whatever length of life was left to her for the glory of God and the good of souls.

SEVEN

Portrait of a Soul

Edel made her first visit to Lourdes in August 1934. The occasion was the pilgrimage organised by the Legion of Mary for its members from all over the world, a sign of the rapid expansion that had taken place during the preceding six years.

The first overseas Praesidium of the Legion was formed in Scotland in 1928. The Legion spread to England in 1929, to India and the U.S.A. in 1931, to the West Indies and Australia in 1932, to New Zealand in 1933. By 1934 a start had been made also in Africa, with Praesidia in both Nigeria and South Africa. There was much to be thankful for and much to be prayed for, and Lourdes, the world's best known centre of Marian devotion, seemed just the place for it.

The journey from Dublin to Lourdes meant two days of gruelling travel. First there was the sea-journey from Dublin to Holyhead, then the long train-ride across England to the Channel ports. Then came a second sea-journey to France and a second and even longer train-ride to Lourdes. Edel made the wise decision to travel as one of the invalids. They were accommodated in special compartments on the train, where they could rest under the supervision of doctors and nurses. Wheelchairs were provided to avoid the need of long walks on quays and station platforms. In Lourdes, they were housed in the building known as the Asile, equipped and staffed to cater for invalids.

It was late at night when they reached their destination. Edel described their arrival in a letter to her friend from the sanatorium, Winnie Leavy.

> Lourdes – the first one sees at about 10.45 p.m. from the train is a red cross (like fire) away on the top of the mountains. It is on the Pic de Jer and, silhouetted against the sky and mountains, is very striking. As one gets nearer one sees an old castle on a height. This is floodlighted, which throws it into relief.

The grotto is next to describe – very simple – Inchicore is a good replica. To the left are the piscinae or baths. The statue of Our Lady in the niche is not very beautiful – it is very weather beaten – underneath it as at Inchicore is the altar, to the right of which burns a large candle holder, the centre of which holds a very large wax candle. To the left of the grotto hang the crutches etc.

Edel was determined to take part in all the exercises of the pilgrimage. Every day she went to the baths, to be wrapped in a cold wet sheet and lowered into the healing waters by the attendant women. Every afternoon, she took her place in Rosary Square among the wheelchairs and stretchers of the invalids to receive the blessing of the sick.

It proved impossible, however, to confine her to a wheelchair. One afternoon she borrowed a badge and cloak from a friend and walked in the Blessed Sacrament procession. Another day she joined with the rest of the Legion group and walked to the Bishop's house to meet him and receive his blessing. On the way back under the blaze of the midday sun she became weak and had to be helped to the side of the street. She admitted that in her anxiety to be in time for the Bishop, she had left the Asile without her breakfast. She recovered quickly and returned to Dublin physically exhausted but spiritually refreshed.

Her friendship with Mary Walls continued to strengthen and it is to Mary that we owe most of our knowledge about her at this time. Mary was a constant companion, a kindred soul, an acute and sympathetic observer, a person of great insight and deep spirituality. Moreover, she had the same spiritual adviser as Edel. She could reasonably assume that the direction he gave her did not differ greatly from the direction he gave to Edel.

Father Boylan had a great respect for the religious life, especially the contemplative life. His two sisters both entered contemplative orders, and his brother Kevin became a Cistercian, later achieving fame as Father Eugene Boylan, Abbot of Mount Melleray and author of *This Tremendous Lover* and other spiritual books. Father Dermot himself was ordained for the diocese of Dublin but he felt himself increasingly attracted away from the diocesan priesthood towards a life of contemplation.

This attraction influenced the way he dealt with his penitents. He encouraged them to realise in their lives the ideals of the religious life, in so far as this could be done by a lay person. He held before them the three religious vows of poverty, chastity and obedience as guidelines towards a life of perfection in the world. He urged them to devote as much time as possible to prayer, taking into account the actual life situation in which they found themselves. Mary describes how this applied to Edel.

> She tried to follow as closely as possible the rule of life laid down by her director. Mass, meditation, visit to the Blessed Sacrament, rosary and, I think, the Little Office of Our Lady, spiritual reading and the habitual practice of recollection in the presence of God, were the daily nourishment of her interior life. Even in company with others, there was in her demeanour a certain air of recollection that is difficult to describe, because she was in no way closed in on herself. She was always attentive to others and she seemed completely forgetful of herself, full of courtesy and sympathy, bright, humorous, full of life; and yet her gaiety never gave the impression of dissipation. You felt in her a supernatural radiance which seemed to come from the presence of the divine Guest of whom she was always aware. It was extraordinary how she managed to fuse together two aspects of her life that seemed completely opposed to one another.

Father Boylan proposed poverty, chastity and obedience as ideals rather than formal commitments. The obedience he asked for was primarily to himself as spiritual director. Unlike some more autocratic directors, he did not allow his directees to make a vow of obedience to him. But he did require them to submit their intellects and wills to him as the representative of God, which is the essence of religious obedience. Edel was happy to do this, as obedience had been one of the things that had attracted her to the convent. It was a result of her obedience to him that she modified her penances and probably lengthened her life.

Chastity was a virtue in which she needed little schooling. All those who knew her were struck by her balance and discernment in sexual matters. In her words, in her actions, in her dealings with others, she manifested purity without prudishness. In this regard, she became to some extent the director of her director. Father Boylan had been accustomed to warn his penitents against dances as an occasion of sin. He modified his views when he found that someone with as delicate a conscience as Edel could enjoy dancing as a normal and innocent recreation.

On the practice of poverty he laid great stress. Here too Edel was happy to obey, as Mary Walls recounts.

> I think Edel had made a vow of poverty by which she obliged herself to submit for his approval all expenses she wished to incur for her own needs, except in the case of little things such as stockings. It was rather the sum that was fixed. Through obedience on this point, she provided herself once with a winter outfit so dowdy and unsuitable to her that the family objected.
>
> She persisted in dressing like that all that winter, but at Easter she blossomed out in a very fashionable and becoming ensemble. When I met her thus attired I exclaimed in surprise, whereupon she laughed and told me she had yielded to her family's remonstrances. She did not think she could continue to inflict on them the displeasure she had caused them by her winter outfit. She had probably come to an agreement on this point with her director.

The relation between the director and the directee is always a delicate one. Father Boylan was following the received wisdom of the time in laying down strong and clear guidelines for Edel. She too was following the received wisdom in obeying them even against her own better judgement. In religious houses, novices were sometimes asked to perform pointless or even ridiculous actions in order to test their obedience and humility. Edel's winter outfit may have been a test of this nature. But what was understandable within the walls of a novitiate could be misunderstood by the world. It is doubtful if Edel did any good to herself or anyone else by walking around the streets of Dublin looking like Mary Poppins.

There were other small signs of tension between Edel and her director. One Saturday, after she and Mary had both been to confession to him, she seemed a little upset. When Mary questioned her, her only answer was, 'I wish he'd leave me alone.' It was evident that he was asking her to do something she did not feel happy about. And when he left Ireland soon afterwards and Mary bemoaned their loss, Edel smiled and said it could all be for the best.

Father Boylan's departure came as a result of his decision to become a Carthusian. Founded by St Bruno in 1084, the Carthusians are the most austere of the Church's contemplative orders. They live in monasteries but spend much of their time in solitude, combining the vocations of the monk and the hermit. As they had no house in Ireland, Father Boylan entered the monastery in Parkminster, near London. He spent the rest of his life as Father Stephen Mary and was responsible for founding the first Carthusian monastery in America.

His friends in the Legion organised a farewell party for him in the Regina Coeli Hostel. It was one of the few occasions when Mary saw Edel in bad humour. It was partly due to the loss of someone who, in spite of occasional differences, had been a great support and inspiration to her. Furthermore, the group who were pouring out the tea contrived to omit Edel, fearing that the heavy catering teapots would be too much for her frail strength. Edel felt rebuffed and became uncharacteristically silent. Mary went over to her and said, 'Edel, I'm surprised at you,' to which she answered with some heat, 'You may be,' obviously disappointed at being prevented from doing this last service for her director. The mood soon passed off and on the way home she was her usual self.

The two of them now began their search for a new director. Mary consulted a friend who lived nearby, Mary Martin, whom she considered to be a saint. Miss Martin was later to found the Medical Missionaries of Mary. She put Mary Walls in touch with a very well known priest who impressed her greatly and became her director. But Edel was unwilling to see him. She said she had had dealings with him when he was teaching her brother in Blackrock College and had never felt at ease with him. Mary does not name him, but her description could only apply to Father Edward Leen, an eminent writer and preacher who inspired worship in some and terror in others.

Miss Martin was unexpectedly philosophical about Edel's decision. She told Mary it was her belief that Edel was one of those rare souls who do not need a director because they are under the direct guidance of the Holy Spirit. She added these words which made a deep and lasting impression on Mary. 'I have observed Miss Quinn. She is very near to God.'

Not long after this Mary made the decision that was to shape the rest of her life. For some time she had felt the same call as Father Boylan to a life of solitude and contemplation. Like him, she believed she could answer this call only by becoming a Carthusian. She does not tell us how she broke the news to Edel or what her reaction was. Knowing her friend so intimately, Edel can hardly have been greatly surprised but this did nothing to lessen the sadness at being separated from so close a friend.

Together they discussed the arrangements for her departure. Mary had received a prospectus from the convent which listed the qualities looked for in a future nun. She had always been by far the more serious-minded of the two and so she was somewhat taken aback to find that one of the desired qualities was gaiety. 'I wonder if they will find me gay enough?' she asked Edel. She answered, 'Oh yes, I thing you'll do,' and added reassuringly, 'You have improved in that respect since I made your acquaintance.'

It was only in the last days before she left for the convent in Italy that Mary realised how much Edel valued her friendship. She had often noticed that when they were together and a third friend joined them, Edel would welcome the newcomer warmly and make a space for her between them. Mary felt that this was because these others were closer friends of Edel than she was.

On her last evening in Dublin, Mary was in the Quinn home on Monkstown Road. When Edel was momentarily out of the room, Mrs Quinn told Mary how much Edel was going to miss her. 'Oh, I don't think so,' Mary answered. 'She has Mona and Muriel and all her other friends.' 'Oh no,' said Mrs Quinn. 'The other evening she was talking to me about you and about your going away and she said to me, "She is the only friend I have." ' Mary took this to mean that none of her other friendships touched the same depth and intimacy as this one. And she understood for the first time that when Edel made room for others she acted from grace not from nature. No-one must ever feel unwanted or second-best in her company.

Edel was among the family and friends who saw Mary off at Dun Laoghaire. She was as usual perfectly self-controlled. But a few days earlier she had given Mary a book of the Little Flower's writings. In it she placed a picture on which she wrote the date of the departure with the words '*Fiat voluntas tua*' – 'Your will be done.'

On her way to Italy, Mary spent one night in a religious house. A nun there handed her a postcard with a slightly disapproving look. It was from Edel and bore a message of good wishes on one side. On the other side, instead of the expected view or holy picture, there was one of those Donald McGill-type drawings which usually featured enormous domineering wives and small hen-pecked husbands with red noses and bowler hats. It showed a man answering his front door to a rag-and-bone merchant. 'Have you any old thing that you want to get rid of?' asks the dealer. 'No, not today,' the man answers, 'my wife is not at home.' It was just what Mary needed on a night when she felt closer to tears than to laughter.

Mary and Edel never saw one another again, though they continued to correspond up to the end. Thirty years later Mary wrote her recollections of her friend. She was now Sister Mary Celestine, Mother Prioress of the Carthusian Convent of St Francis at Giaveno in Northern Italy. She wrote them in French for the Postulator of Edel's cause in Rome, since English was not apparently understood there. Later she produced a shorter version in English, which was published as a booklet under the title *I Knew Edel Quinn, by an Irish Carthusian Nun*. Good though the English version is, the original French is even better. It is from the French version that this long last extract is taken, an attempt at describing Edel's spiritual life.

Edel revealed nothing about her own interior life. When the two of us were alone, she spoke willingly about the interior life in general; and it was only by drawing conclusions from her conversation and seeing the effects in her life that I was able to come to some idea of her life of union with God. In our intimate conversations I learnt how she loved to live in silent communion with the Blessed Trinity in the depths of her soul. She had a deep understanding of the mysteries of the Faith and she loved especially those that dealt with the indwelling of the Three Divine Persons in the soul and also with the Divine Immensity which she understood in its purely spiritual dimension.

We often spoke together about this and it was clear to me that her conception of God was free from all limitations of time and place, and that she was capable of entering into contemplation of the Divine Being in its Three Persons without the help of figures or images drawn from the world of the senses. This is why she was very fond of some passages from Louis de Blois. She also liked *Christ in His Mysteries* by Dom Marmion and she particularly liked his treatment of the life and relationships within the Blessed Trinity. I cannot remember the exact words she used in talking about this; but I do remember that she spoke about it with such clarity that I got the impression she had received infused illuminations and an experimental knowledge of the Divine Presence in her soul.

Her way of understanding the Sacraments and all the Mysteries was also very spiritual. She loved Dom Vonier's book *A Key to the Doctrine of the Eucharist* because it explained how the Mass and the Sacraments have the privilege of overcoming the obstacles of time and place. She attended Mass with a most lively faith in the sacramental presence of the sacrifice of the cross. She once sent me a picture which showed Jesus on the cross in a cloud above the altar, seeming to envelop the sacred host as it was elevated at the consecration of the Mass, and she wrote to me that this was her favourite picture of the Mass, adding that she loved to attend Mass every day. In fact, she went to Mass whenever she had the opportunity.

Her ideal of life was St Paul's 'Vivo jam non ego, vivit vero in me Christus' [I live, now not I, but Christ lives in me] as developed in the little book *One with Jesus* by De Jaegher, but she joined with it the practice of *The True Devotion to Mary* taught by St Louis-Marie Grignion de Montfort. To this she consecrated herself with all her heart. She had a truly filial devotion to the Blessed Virgin and she spoke about her with a deep love. She had a leaflet giving an English translation of a poem by St Thérèse of the Child Jesus *Why I love Thee, Mary* and she was very fond of it.

No-one knew Edel better than Mary Walls. The friendship between the two was a friendship made in heaven. When they met without the presence of a third party, their talk was about the things of the spirit. They shared books, thoughts, insights, illuminations. They grew together and helped one another to grow.

Mary was the one who penetrated furthest beyond the barrier of Edel's privacy and reserve. When she wrote her recollections it was after thirty years of praying and reflecting, thirty years of studying mystical theology and experiencing it. She does not capture the whole of Edel's soul for us but she comes closer than anyone else.

EIGHT

Envoy to Africa

Slowly and almost by stealth, Edel resumed her involvement with the work of the Legion of Mary. She stayed on as a member of the Praesidium in Temple Hill and resisted the temptation to join a more active Praesidium, no doubt out of deference to the wishes of her family. Nevertheless, she made no secret of her frustration. 'You have me sitting up in a coffin,' she complained to her Legion friends.

With her mother watching over her anxiously and insisting on early bedtimes, she found little time for Legion work on weekday evenings. It was easier at weekends. She joined in outings, she went on weekend retreats, she attended the monthly meeting of the Concilium, the supreme governing body of the Legion. She took part in extension work, which meant travelling to different parts of Ireland, telling priests and religious about the Legion and helping to set up new Praesidia.

All her best friends were now drawn from the Legion. The three who were closest to her were Muriel Wailes, Mona McCarthy and Emma Bodkin. Frank Duff christened them The Gang and the name stuck. Edel enjoyed their company and there was always plenty of laughter when she was around. But there were areas of her life that she could not share with them in the way she had shared with Mary Walls. No one could take Mary's place.

One day Edel and Muriel were in Grafton Street and found themselves outside Ross's photographic studio. On an impulse, Muriel suggested they go in and have their portraits taken. Edel agreed and they sat for two double portraits, head and shoulder shots of the two of them sitting side by side. Both were duly touched up before being printed.

Years later, after Edel's death, the Legion were looking for a good quality photograph for publicity purposes. They found plenty of snapshots but no studio portraits except the two taken in Ross's. Muriel was carefully blotted out and the two photographs were reproduced in many forms, eventually becoming the official portraits of Edel Quinn. The choice was unfortunate. All the character, all the humour and playfulness were missing from her face. 'I never saw her look like that in her life,' said Frank Duff.

Some of the blame may be laid on the atmosphere of the tudio. The formality of the occasion and the long exposure time neec d in those days tended to freeze people's faces into masks. But even more blame must laid on the photographer's ill-advised attempts at improvement. As part of the touching-up process, he brushed out the lines and creases on her face, including the pouches beneath her eyes and the laughter lines beside her mouth. The result is a vacuous china doll, drained of individuality and humanity.

It is interesting to recall that much the same thing happened to St Thérèse of Lisieux after she died. The nuns in Lisieux, with the best of intentions, not only re-wrote her autobiography; they also re-drew her face. Her eyes, pouched like Edel's, and her pleasant round face were re-cast in a form thought more suitable for statues and holy pictures and stained glass windows.

As Vice-President of her Praesidium, Edel was entitled to attend the meetings of the Legion's Concilium, which normally took place once a month on a Sunday evening. At one of these meetings in the early part of 1936 she heard about preparations for an extension drive which was being planned by the Legion in England and Wales. They intended to send teams into different parts of the country to promote interest in the Legion and to prepare the ground for new Praesidia. Each team was to consist of two Legionaries, one English and one Irish. They were looking for volunteers from Ireland to take part in the work.

Edel and Muriel had been planning two weeks holiday in Wales. On the way home in Emma Bodkins' car, Edel said to Muriel, 'What about it?' 'What about what?' 'What about Menevia?' Muriel knew that that was the end of the holiday. They went to Frank Duff and volunteered for the work.

Frank found himself in a quandary. He knew that Edel was far from cured and he hesitated to expose her to two weeks of constant travel and stress. But she could be very persuasive when she made up her mind and he found it difficult to resist her arguments. Eventually he allowed her to go, but only on one condition. She was to be teamed not with an English Legionary but with Muriel Wailes. He was confident that Muriel would be a restraining influence. 'If the Legion required them to miss their dinner,' he told a friend, 'Edel would, Muriel would not.'

He spoke to Muriel separately and told her that he was appointing her to be Edel's guardian angel. She was to bring Edel home if she showed any sign of ill-health. By this stage, Muriel was beginning to have second thoughts. She had never spoken in public before and was afraid that she would be a failure. Frank encouraged her in his own unique way. 'Do your best,' he told her, 'and always remember that the work is too important for Our Lady to allow the likes of you to make a mess of it.'

They were assigned to work in the diocese of Menevia, which covered north and central Wales, a mountainous and sparsely populated area. It was close to Ireland both in its location and in its strong Celtic identity, but it had been bypassed by the Irish emigrants of the nineteenth century who did so much to build up the Catholic Church in Britain. The proportion of Catholics in the population of Menevia was one of the lowest in the country.

They arrived in mid-May and made their base in Chester, which was actually in England, in the diocese of Shrewsbury. They were courteously received by Dr Moriarty, Bishop of Shrewsbury, and they noted that in spite of his Irish name he spoke with a very English accent. He told them of all the organisations that had been tried and had failed, but gave them leave to see if they could be more successful with the Legion of Mary.

They visited a number of parishes in Chester before going on to Menevia, where they also had the Bishop's approval. Their work consisted mainly in calling at the houses of parish priests, telling them about the Legion and trying to persuade them to start a Praesidium among the layfolk of their parish. It was tiring work, repeating the same explanations over and over again, answering the same questions, countering the same objections. Many of the priests appeared disheartened. They had tried so many other initiatives without success: why should this one be any different? Muriel could understand their feeling of powerlessness. 'It's possible to cope with hostility,' she said afterwards, 'but it's a very hard thing to face complete indifference.'

The greater the obstacles, the more Edel blossomed. Far from being exhausted, she seemed to thrive on the challenge. 'We have been all over the globe,' she wrote on a postcard to a friend, 'made headquarters Chester and went over as far as Bangor (next stop Holyhead) a few times. We have four Praesidia, two started and two before we leave and a promise of others.' Her one regret was that she would have to return to Ireland with the work barely started. It was not enough for her to sow the seed of the Legion: she needed to be there to coax it into life and growth. She began to talk to Muriel about giving up her job in Dublin and taking one in Chester. She would have her evenings and weekends free for Legion work and would be able to follow up the contacts she had made. By the time she returned to Ireland, the idea had hardened into a resolution.

They went to see Frank Duff in his little office on the upper floor of the Regina Coeli Hostel. Muriel met someone in the hostel who delayed her and Edel went on up alone. A few minutes later she came racing down the stairs, her face alight with joy. 'What did he say?' Muriel asked her. 'He said would it make any difference if I went to Africa instead of Wales,' she answered. 'I said it wouldn't make the slightest difference.'

Frank Duff had just received a letter from Ruby Dennison, the young Irishwoman who had gone as Legion envoy to South Africa. The Legion was now firmly established there and the prospects for expansion were excellent. But the vast distances involved made it impossible for her to visit more than a fraction of the missions. She begged the Legion to send out another envoy to help in the work.

Edel's plan to go to Chester came like an answer to prayer. If she was willing to go to Britain, perhaps she might be equally willing to go to South Africa. There was no doubt about her ability, about her motivation, about her will-power. Even her health seemed to be less of a problem than before. She had stood up surprisingly well to the rigours of Menevia. The warm dry climate of South Africa would suit her far better than either Ireland or England, with their long damp cold winters. When Frank decided to ask her, he had a good idea how she would react. 'Never have I seen a happier person,' he commented later.

Her next step was to persuade her family. She no longer needed to worry about their financial situation, as her three sisters and her brother were all now working. She was always good at persuading others when she put her mind to it, and she managed to secure her parents' assent if not their whole-hearted approval. She laid particular stress on the wholesome climate of South Africa and played down the hard work and wearisome travel involved. At the same time, she promised that she would come back after three years if her mother asked her.

It proved much more difficult to get the approval of her fellow members of the Legion of Mary. They knew exactly what would be involved in the work of a Legion envoy. They knew about the hours and days of travel under the African sun. They knew about the early mornings and the late nights and the endless meetings and interviews that so often proved fruitless. They knew about the frustrations and disappointments that so sorely tested the heart and the will. Edel loved to repeat a phrase she had heard in a retreat: 'It is the will, the will, the will, that matters.' No-one doubted her will-power. But no amount of will-power could restore a ravaged lung or rebuild a shattered physique.

A revolt began to spread among her friends in the Legion, which meant practically everybody involved with the Legion in Dublin.

She was well known, well respected, well loved. Her courage in the face of ill-health was widely admired. Her dedication to the ideals of the Legion was legendary. None of those who knew her could doubt that she had made the decision to go to Africa freely and consciously. But they felt that she had made a hasty and unwise decision and that she had been manipulated into doing so by Frank Duff. It was one of the worst ordeals of Frank's life. He stood firm under a battery of criticism, absolutely convinced of the rightness of what he was doing. 'She is like a wild bird,' he said. 'You cannot keep her in a cage.' He admitted that she probably had not long to live. But why not let her live those last years or months or days the way she wanted to live them, doing the work of God? Why try to protect her from a death that was inevitable? 'You don't hold an umbrella over someone who is already soaked,' he kept insisting.

The question was put on the agenda for the next meeting of the Concilium. It would have to be decided by a vote of all those entitled to attend. Those who were opposed to Edel going began to gather their forces and to use very emotive language in their quest for supporters. Frank Duff was singled out for special attack and accused of sending an innocent girl to her death. He got some inkling of how high feelings were running when he had a chance meeting with Mona McCarthy, one of Edel's closest friends. He offered her his hand but she refused to take it. 'I can't shake hands with you,' she declared dramatically, 'because your hands are covered in blood!'

He received a further blow when the opposition gained the support of Father Elias Magennis. Father Magennis was a former General of the Carmelite Order, a man of strong views and forceful personality, and an ardent supporter of the Legion of Mary. He was much admired and respected in Legion circles and it seemed as if his intervention must be decisive. 'We're lost,' said Frank when he heard the news.

There was an exceptionally full attendance at the fateful meeting of the Concilium. It was held as usual at 8 o'clock on Sunday evening in a large and rather shabby room in the Regina Coeli Hostel. Frank Duff was in the chair. The proceedings began with the saying of the Rosary. The minutes of the previous meeting were read and signed. The reports from various parts of the world were listened to and discussed.

Then came the item on the agenda that everyone was waiting for, the appointment of Sister Quinn as an envoy to Africa. The chairman's heart sank when Father Magennis rose to address the meeting. He spoke with great vehemence about the folly of sending Edel on so difficult and dangerous a mission. He described in graphic detail the harsh conditions she would have to contend with. He quoted from the experience of missionaries and other experts, among them Cardinal Hinsley who had visited missions in many parts of Africa on behalf of the Vatican. If they wanted to send an envoy, said Father Magennis, they should send a strong man, not a girl in such a delicate state of health. He seemed to be carrying the whole meeting with him when he was halted by an unexpected intervention.

Up to this point the victim herself had not said a word. Edel always felt a little nervous about speaking to large gatherings, and no-one could remember her ever saying anything at the Concilium. But when she saw the opportunity of going to Africa slipping away from her she forgot her nervousness. She stood up and said she had made her decision to go to Africa with her eyes open. She knew the situation, she had considered the matter fully, she had been made well aware of all the difficulties involved. 'I don't think I'm going on any picnic,' she said.

The thought of a picnic proved too much for Father Magennis's sense of humour. 'Picnic! Picnic!' he roared genially. 'You'll make a nice picnic for someone out there!' There was a burst of laughter from the audience. Then Frank came in quickly. 'I call on all of you to witness,' he said, 'that the picnic will not be a very substantial one.' This time the laughter came in gales. The thought of the emaciated Edel as the main course of anybody's picnic was irresistibly comic.

All the tension suddenly disappeared. They saw Edel in a new light. She was not a helpless victim being sent to a dreadful fate. She was a courageous, humorous, clear-sighted young woman, who knew exactly what she was doing and why she was doing it. She did not deserve pity. She deserved support.

The chairman put the question to a vote. A sea of hands arose in favour. He asked if anyone was opposed. No-one was, not even Father Magennis. The meeting went on to the next item on the agenda. Edel sat quietly in her place. By the unanimous vote of the Concilium, she was now the Legion of Mary's new envoy for Africa.

There was an unexpected sequel to the Concilium meeting two evenings later. Father Magennis was spiritual director of a Legion Praesidium which met on Tuesday nights in the Carmelite Priory in Whitefriar Street. Among those present was Emmie Colgan and she has left us a description of what happened that night.

Edel appeared quite unexpectedly, it wasn't her Praesidium, and she went over to the priest quickly and went down on her two knees in front of him. You could see she was upset. 'I want to ask forgiveness for Sunday,' she began. We all realised at once what was troubling her. The poor thing felt that by winning in the Concilium against Father Magennis's strong opposition she had publicly humiliated him and that this demanded an apology.

Poor Father Magennis was really a kind-hearted man and he was so touched at the sight of her kneeling in front of him that he was nearly in tears. Everyone else was the same. Father Magennis lifted her up and said he was sorry himself about the position he had taken up on Sunday. 'You must go, Edel,' he said. 'You will do great work for God and he will help you. I will never forget you in my daily Mass.'

Edel stayed until after the allocutio. Before she went, she hugged and kissed everybody there. All the girls loved her. I don't think there was ever a Legionary who was loved so much.

NINE

The Voyage

It was some time before it became clear to Edel what precise part of Africa she was going to. The original plan was that she would go to South Africa and join forces with Ruby Dennison, the resident envoy. Then somebody had what seemed to be a bright idea. Instead of going directly to South Africa, she could start in North Africa and work her way down. She could disembark at Alexandria, travel through Egypt and Sudan into the British colonies of East and central Africa and finally end up in the dominion of South Africa, having established the Legion of Mary all along the way.

A little inquiry soon showed how impracticable this was. Egypt and Sudan were predominantly Muslim countries. There were large areas in which there was no Christian presence. There would be no missionaries to offer her help and hospitality, no Catholic lay men and women to be recruited for the Legion. In addition, the roads were often primitive and there were parts, especially in the vast and underpopulated Sudan, where there were no roads at all. While this was being pondered over, Frank Duff received a letter from Bishop John William Heffernan, Vicar Apostolic of Zanzibar, which decided the matter. It was dated 14 September 1936, the Feast of the Exaltation of the Holy Cross and Edel's twenty-ninth birthday.

You propose to send Miss Quinn inland from Alexandria? With all due respect, I suggest that you get in touch with my missionaries coming out in October, and that she come with them and with the Loreto nuns (from Rathfarnham) coming out at the same time. She would land at Mombasa and work her way inland to the Nile and Uganda. Landing here, she would be in touch with scores of priests who know about the Legion: Holy Ghost Fathers, Mill Hill Fathers, White Fathers, and the Loreto nuns. I ask it as a favour that you allow us to work out her itinerary, and that you let her travel with our people, following the Red Sea route. They are due to sail at the end of October.

It was an offer that could not be refused. Bishop Heffernan's Vicariate was named after the island of Zanzibar, but his residence and centre of administration were in Nairobi, the capital city of the colony of Kenya and the political and commercial hub of British East Africa. It was the ideal spot from which to undertake the setting up of the Legion in all that vast area. From Kenya she could continue on through Uganda, Tanganyika, Nyasaland, Northern and Southern Rhodesia, and finally reach South Africa. They all formed part of the British Empire and they all had English as their official language. Most important of all, they were criss-crossed by a network of missions with many Irish priests, sisters and brothers, who would welcome her and help her on her way. Bishop Heffernan's offer was gratefully accepted and arrangements were made for Edel to form part of the group of missionaries on their journey to Mombasa.

In the meantime, she had made another visit to Lourdes. The second Legion pilgrimage took place in mid-August and once again she joined it, this time as an ordinary pilgrim, not as an invalid. As usual she was more concerned with the needs of others than with her own. One of her fellow-pilgrims was Winnie Leavy, whom she had met while they were both patients in Newcastle Sanatorium. Winnie was still sick and, with the death of her father, her family had fallen on hard times. Edel arranged for her to go as an invalid and even provided her with clothing and toiletries. She was unfailing in her attention to her all during the journey.

Another pilgrim she devoted much of her time to was Tim Barry, a young auxiliary member of the Legion, who was also suffering from tuberculosis. He was a neighbour of hers from Monkstown and had worked as gardener in the Carmelite Convent in Blackrock, where she and her mother often attended Mass. He died soon afterwards. Winnie recovered and attributed her cure to Edel's prayers.

She took part in all the exercises of the pilgrimage and added a few of her own. She spent one whole night in prayer at the Grotto with a few other Legionaries. Her only complaint was that the men coming to sweep it out in the morning had distracted her from her prayers.

Only once did she show signs of weakness, in circumstances similar to the previous pilgrimage. The pilgrims were received by the Bishop one morning and Edel was presented to him as the future envoy to Africa. During the lengthy reception, which took place in the open, she fainted and admitted afterwards that she had come straight from Mass without eating any breakfast. It seems to have been an isolated incident and she looks well enough in some photographs taken during the pilgrimage, though noticeably thin.

On her return to Dublin, the final preparations had to be made for her voyage. The missionaries were due to travel from London on 29 October on board the M.V. *Llangibby Castle*. There was a last minute scare when it was discovered that the ship was completely booked out. Then there was a cancellation. It was a first class cabin and cost £70, which was considered very expensive, but there was no alternative. Frank Duff was secretly glad, as it meant that Edel could travel in some comfort. Edel did not share his joy. Her attitude

Edel, in Dublin, September or October 1936.

was that of the saintly English priest Father Ignatius Spencer, who was asked why he always travelled third class and replied, 'Because there is no fourth.'

There was a long round of goodbyes to be said, including several farewell functions and parties. Edel found these extremely trying. She hated the limelight and found it hard to keep smiling through the barrage of compliments and congratulations. A young student nurse, Madeleine Gallagher, saw her for the first and only time at a meeting of the Concilium on the eve of her departure. To her youthful eyes, the room seemed to be filled with fat middle-aged ladies, all of them fussing importantly around. She asked the cause of the commotion and was told that Edel Quinn was leaving for Africa. While she was wondering which of the ladies was Edel Quinn, someone pointed out the real Edel, sitting quietly and patiently, almost invisible in the midst of the turmoil. Suddenly she caught Madeleine's eye and seemed to guess her thoughts. She smiled at her and raised her eyes to heaven in mock resignation.

I think of her as a very pretty girl with huge big blue sparkling eyes, that looked as though they were laughing across the room at me, when she caught my eye. And the gentleness of her – I felt that if I had been in her position, I'd have shoved all those ladies away and said, 'All right, that's it.'

The abiding impression that remained with her was of Edel's sheer ordinariness. 'I'm very consoled that a saint could look so ordinary, so pretty and so young, just like any of us, any of the young girls that were there.'

One important visit she made was to the Nunciature in the Phoenix Park. Archbishop Antonio Riberi was staying there on a brief visit as guest of the Papal Nuncio. Dr Riberi had recently been appointed Apostolic Delegate to Africa in succession to Cardinal Hinsley and he was anxious to meet the new Legion envoy. He himself had once spent four years in Dublin as a junior official in the Nunciature and he had come to know and esteem the Legion of

Mary during that time. He invited Edel, Frank Duff and John Nagle to meet him in the Nunciature and he promised to send letters to all the Bishops in East Africa recommending Edel and the Legion.

On 24 October, her last day in Ireland, she went to early Mass as usual. Then she disappeared from home, only returning in the evening a short time before she was due to leave. Evidently she felt unable to cope with a long day full of heavy emotion. A wild last-minute flurry of packing kept her occupied until it was time to leave the house and say her last goodbye to her mother, who felt unable to face the ordeal of the quayside.

She took the night boat to England from the North Wall in Dublin. The rest of her family were there to see her off, together with a large group of friends from the Legion of Mary and elsewhere. She remained remarkably cheerful and calm during the farewells. A number of Legionaries travelled with her to London, among them Frank Duff and John Nagle. John (or Jack, as he was more familiarly known) was now President of the Concilium but the real authority still remained with Frank Duff.

The few days in London were put to good use. She visited the Mill Hill Fathers and the White Fathers, both active in East Africa, and the Archbishop of Westminster, Cardinal Hinsley, former Apostolic Delegate to Africa. All of them promised their support and their prayers.

One day was devoted to a visit to the Carthusian monastery in Parkminster. Accompanied by Frank Duff, she saw Father Dermot Boylan, now Father Stephen Mary, who during his time in Dublin had been spiritual director to several Praesidia and had conducted Legion retreats, in addition to being her own spiritual director. She asked him and the community to pray for the success of her mission, which they willingly agreed to do. Father Boylan and the Novice Master each promised to say one Mass every month for her and her work, as long as she continued in Africa.

The ship was due to sail on Thursday 29 October. Some more Legion friends came over from Dublin on Wednesday to give her a rousing send-off. A farewell function was held that evening in the new Legion hostel at Haverstock Hill. It proved a little premature, as the departure of the ship was unexpectedly delayed by a day.

Two of the Legionaries, Jack Nagle and Emma Bodkin, could not wait over the extra day and returned to Dublin. They had come to see Edel off. Instead she saw them off. It proved to be a memorable experience. When the two of them arrived to take their pre-booked places in the train at Euston Station, they found that their compartment had been lavishly decorated with streamers and wedding bells as if for a honeymoon couple. They had barely taken their seats when Edel and her fellow-conspirators produced packets of confetti and showered them generously with the contents, to the delight of the other passengers and the extreme embarrassment of the ill-matched couple themselves (Jack was 30 years of age, Emma 43). Emma did her best to brazen it out but John took refuge behind the evening paper and did not emerge until the train reached Holyhead.

Friday 30 October dawned bright and sunny and calm. The party travelled by train to the docks at Tilbury where the *Llangibby Castle* was berthed. The ship, a 12,000 ton liner, looked enormous. Passengers were allowed to bring their friends on board so they all trooped up the gangway, wandered around the decks and inspected Edel's first-class cabin. In addition to Frank Duff, the group included Father Creedon, spiritual director of the Concilium, Mona McCarthy, Muriel Wailes, Celia Shaw, Eileen O'Connor, Mary Rowe, and the president of the English Senatus, Mrs De la Mare. Various snapshots were taken, including one of Edel and Frank which still survives. Frank is smiling his usual bland smile. Edel is smiling too, but she cannot conceal the lines of pain about her eyes and mouth.

She allowed Muriel Wailes a glimpse of her true feelings. 'Don't you break down,' she said to her. 'If you break, I'll break.'

'You'll be back shortly,' said Muriel.

'I'm not coming back,' Edel replied. 'I'm not putting the Concilium to the expense of sending me out only to come back after three years. I'm not coming back. Missionaries don't come back.'

The ship's siren sounded, a sign that those who were not travelling must leave the boat. Edel stood near the gangway and embraced her friends as they left. She was the only who was not crying openly. They stood on the quayside and waved as the band played 'God Save the King' and the ship pulled slowly away. They all felt that they would never see her again.

Edel's feelings can best be judged from a letter she wrote to Frank Duff shortly after the ship left port. She used it to say to him some of the things she could not say face to face.

I could not say 'thanks' as I was afraid of breaking down, perhaps; but it was good to feel one is trusted and it will be a help in the days to come.

I would like you to remember always, whatever happens, that I am *glad* you gave me the opportunity of going. I realize it is a privilege and also that only you persisted I personally would never have been sent. I only hope I do not fail the Legion when the work comes to be done. I am counting on all the prayers to counteract that danger. Whatever be the consequence, *rejoice* you had the courage to emulate Our Lord, in His choice of weak things, in faith. Any sorrow to others was worth it, remember; I know that you felt pretty badly the fact that others were suffering.

Have no regrets. I am not going to refer to this again. I am glad you let me go – the others will be glad later.

Very sincere thanks,

Pray for

Edel.

There is much in that letter that is typical of Edel: the courtesy and gratitude, the delicacy with which they are expressed, the quiet confidence that is based on the prayers of others rather than her own strength. Most typical of all is one phrase: 'I am not going to refer to this again.' On the occasion of a parting which might well be final, she was prepared to tell more than usual of her inmost feelings. He not need fear that the same note would be struck in later letters. It was a unique occasion. It would not happen again.

Before leaving Dublin, Edel had promised to keep a log of her journey to be published in the Legion's new quarterly magazine, *Maria Legionis*. She kept the promise faithfully and the pages of her log record the three-week voyage in great detail. The first few days were the worst. The loneliness of parting from her friends was succeeded by the ordeal of the Bay of Biscay. For two days she was confined to bed, prostrated by sea-sickness, subsisting on a little toast and fruit.

It didn't stop her writing. She answered every one of the innumerable people who had sent her letters, cards, gifts and telegrams, lying on her bunk with her Baby Empire on her chest. The Baby Empire was a new acquisition, a portable typewriter which was to accompany her in all her African journeys. It gave her sterling service right to the end and she referred to it with affection in the last line of her last letter, almost eight years later.

On the first two days, 30 October and 1 November, she tried in spite of her sickness to attend Mass in the saloon but was forced to retire. The third day, All Souls' Day, she managed to remain and was able to join the others at their meals. All the missionaries apart from the eight Loreto Sisters were travelling tourist class. She tried to change to the tourist class but there was no vacancy. She then arranged with the Purser to keep her first class cabin but to have all her meals in the tourist class dining room and to have her deck-chair on the tourist deck. Her embarrassment at travelling first class was a little eased when her cabin was pressed into service as a second chapel.

It is arranged that my 'cell', as they call it, be used for two Masses by the Holy Ghost Fathers. The Tourist Saloon where they all say Mass is very packed and they have to be out of it by 7.30 a.m. So the Mass box is being brought along tonight. Our table on the boat is worth description. It is very long, ten a side. At the head two Anglican brethren (deacons), then three Mill Hill Fathers, then a Catholic lady (nice) and her Protestant husband, then three C.S.Sp. Fathers, other side three more C.S.Sp. Fathers, another man, a Mill Hill Father who has been out for seven years before, myself, two Franciscan Nuns, Anglican clergyman (ordained). We are well rounded off. Four or five more Mill Hill Fathers join us at Genoa.

Edel made good use of the four week on the *Llangibby Castle* by getting to know the priests and nuns and telling them all about the Legion of Mary. By the time she reached her destination she had acquired a network of friends who would be happy to welcome her at their missions and convents all over East Africa.

For all its comfort, life on board ship tended to be monotonous. 'The days seem a succession of meals,' she wrote. 'Bedtime is a relief.' As always, the morning Mass was the highlight of her day. 'Father Wallace and Father Marrinan celebrate and I am the congregation. It is great and I am delighted as I have the job of having everything ready, vestments out and altar prepared when they come along at 6.30.'

The routine was varied by occasional shore visits. Gibraltar did not impress her. The town was not particularly interesting and the cathedral was not really worthy of the name. Palma on the island of Majorca was more to her liking and the fifteenth-century cathedral met with her approval. Outside the harbour she saw British, German and Italian battleships. The men on the German ship paraded in military style while their band played 'God Save the King' in honour of the *Llangibby*. The men on the Italian ship had their week's washing fluttering from clothes-lines on the rear top deck.

There were more visits ashore at Marseilles and Genoa and more churches and cathedrals were seen and commented on. Then Europe was left behind as the ship set off across the Mediterranean for Africa. The sea grew rougher and Edel spent another day in bed. A stowaway who had got on the boat at Genoa was discovered when he took someone else's place at table. The excitement was enjoyed by everyone except the stowaway.

They arrived at Port Said in Egypt on 12 November and the passengers were allowed ashore. It was Edel's first time to stand on African soil.

> Port Said is not very impressive; as usual, palm trees border the street which runs along the quay, and the natives, brown-faced with red fez, are everywhere. One cannot move without being pestered by them to buy Turkish Delight, jewellery or sponges. They offer at fancy prices and usually come down to sixpence in the end. They are very persistent and follow one along the road with their wares, unless a policemen gives them a shout, when they retreat a little, only to return anew to the attack. They speak a mixture of languages and several of them use a Scotch name when addressing one, i.e. Please Mrs MacIntyre, etc. One said to me, 'Please buy, Mrs Harry Lauder' to the intense amusement of the nuns.

Their efforts were not entirely wasted. Mrs Harry Lauder consented to have her picture taken by one of the street photographers. She is looking rather solemn, her face shadowed by a sun-helmet which she may have just bought. Her light coloured dress, on the other hand, is pleasingly feminine if not actually frivolous.

Edel at Port Said, 12 November 1936.

The following two days were spent sailing slowly down the Suez Canal. On Sunday 15 November they put in to Port Sudan and Edel decided she wanted to visit a convent which she had heard about from a friend in Ireland. With some difficulty she managed to locate the convent and she met the sisters and the local priest, all of them Italians. She told them about the Legion and, when they showed interest, she promised to have copies of the Legion Handbook in Italian sent to them from Dublin.

The priest went to prepare for the afternoon Benediction, mentioning that he would only have the six nuns for a congregation. Edel raced back to the boat, where she rounded up 'the two Franciscan nuns, two Mill Hill priests, one Catholic passenger, and four Loreto nuns' and brought them along to the church. They sang the familiar Latin hymns lustily before rushing back to the boat again, happy at having had 'their first Benediction on African soil.'

The boat called in to Aden on the 18th and then continued on the last leg of the journey to Mombasa. The heat was now intense. Ventilators worked overtime, bedclothes were stripped from beds, many people slept on deck at night. It was hard to summon the energy to walk or dance or play deck quoits or do anything except sit in the shade and look at the sea. It was too hot even to write and in Edel's cabin the Baby Empire enjoyed a well-deserved rest. The priests had been teasing her about the number of letters she wrote every day and as the voyage neared its end they reckoned she had written more than a thousand. She did her best to minimise it. 'Some of them were only two or three lines,' she said.

TEN

Selling the Legion

Early in the morning of the 23 November 1936 the *Llangibby* docked in Mombasa. Three hundred of the passengers disembarked, amongst them all the missionaries. Mombasa was the gateway to British East Africa and the starting point of the railway line that led all the way to Uganda in the heart of the African continent.

There was the usual bustle and confusion on the quayside as the passenger's luggage was offloaded, including the heavy trunks marked 'not wanted on voyage' which had been stored in the ship's hold during the journey. Edel negotiated the customs without difficulty and was greeted by some of the local priests, led by Bishop Heffernan himself. His normal residence was in Nairobi but he had come to Mombasa to meet the newcomers and welcome them to Kenya.

Edel had been under the impression that she was to make Mombasa her headquarters, possibly because it was the seat of the Apostolic Delegation for Africa. Bishop Heffernan had a different plan for her. He told her that she was to make Nairobi her base, and to travel there by the afternoon train. Nairobi was the civil and ecclesiastical capital of the country and the most convenient centre from which to undertake her work. As the train was leaving at 4 p.m., it left her only a few hours to see Mombasa and attend to some business matters.

One of the priests drove me round to see the sights and showed me 'the Mission'. All these places and towns call the parochial house, church and schools, the Mission – it takes getting used to. Mombasa was very warm – it was the beginning of the hot season there. But everywhere there was a profusion of gorgeously coloured flowers – trees of them. Then I called on the Apostolic Delegation secretary (Mgr Riberi is the Delegate – I saw him in Dub-

lin, you remember) and also on the bank and got the money transferred ex latter to Nairobi. I had already been to the Post Office to
get my letters and got Mother's mail amongst others. I told P.O.
and gave them form filled in to redirect all my letters to Nairobi.

Her main reason for calling to the Delegation was to ask about
the letter of recommendation which Archbishop Riberi had promised to write for her. She found that he was in West Africa and that
his secretary, Father Engelbert, knew nothing about any letter. This
was a disappointment. She was relying on the letter to get approval
from the bishops of the different places she was to visit. However it
did not affect her work in Nairobi, where she already had Bishop
Heffernan's full support.

The journey from Mombasa to Nairobi was, and no doubt still is,
one of the world's great train journeys. Edel had a second class
ticket but by some accident she found herself in a first class compartment. In the course of eighteen hours the train climbed from sea-
level to a height of 5,500 feet. The first couple of hours gave her a
chance to watch the changing panorama of landscape and people before darkness fell. Then came a leisurely dinner in the luxuriously
appointed dining car, after which she went back to her compartment
and a comfortable berth for the night. The following morning she returned to the dining car for a lavish breakfast. The scene outside had
changed dramatically and the lush vegetation of the coast had given
way to the wide open plains of the uplands. The train finally pulled
in to the station in Nairobi at 10.30 a.m. If she felt uncomfortable at
the luxury of this first African journey, she need not have worried.
She was to more than make up for it in the years to come.

The group of Loreto sisters from the boat had travelled with her
on the train. They were met at the station by two of the local Loreto
community and brought to the convent, where they found all the
school children marshalled in the grounds to give them an official
welcome. The sisters had arranged that Edel would stay with them
for the time being and they provided her with a bedroom and a sitting room, where she could have her meals and do her writing in pri-

vacy. They refused any offer of payment. It was, they said, their contribution to the Legion.

The first few days were spent absorbing a multitude of new impressions. She was charmed by Nairobi, with its modern offices and shops and its profusion of flowers and trees. One of the priests brought her on a trip out of the city to visit a rural mission. Bishop Heffernan's vicariate was in the charge of the Irish Holy Ghost Fathers and she quickly found herself at home with them.

We all sat round a log fire in the open grate and chatted of Blackrock, Rockwell and Dublin! Fancy a log fire in Africa only two degrees away from the equator. It is quite mild – no mosquitoes and no need here of hats or boots – English food.

All the work is done by 'boys' who can be any age from 10 to 80. You just shout 'boy' and they appear. Their dress for house, waiting at table, is white cap – [here she puts in a drawing] that shape always – long white garment reaching to ground and red sash. This in train and everywhere. Bare feet. It is funny having a black hand taking away or putting down a plate. On the roads it is the women who work carrying heavy loads etc. and the Lord and Master walks after her.

Bishop Heffernan stayed on a few days in Mombasa. She could not start work until he arrived but she could and did make soundings among the Catholic population. To her disappointment, she found the general reaction negative.

Pessimistic is a mild term to apply to the lot of them when it comes to organisations and asking them to work; everywhere it is the same, 'You do not know Nairobi,' meets one at every turn. Even Reverend Mother here, who has a fine outlook on things in general, after a mild discussion about the futility of getting anything done here, said after all, 'Our Lord's life was a failure and you need not mind when it happens to you.' If it was not the Legion and one had not heard the like before, retreat would be the solution.

One of the problems was the mixture of races and the difficulty of getting white, brown and black to work together. The Europeans looked down on the Asians and the Asians looked down on the Africans. Each group was suspicious of the other.

The Europeans, mostly British and Irish, were involved either in administration or in farming. They had a high standard of living and a rather lower standard of morality. The Asians in the Catholic Church were represented mainly by immigrants from Goa, the Portuguese enclave in India. These Goans were business and professional people, shopkeepers, doctors, lawyers, but the Europeans did not regard them as equals. There were hotels and clubs and restaurants where no Asian was admitted. The Africans, who made up the vast majority of the population, were at the bottom of the social pecking order. They worked as labourers and servants for their colonial masters and were known simply as 'the natives'. But the natives were becoming restless and were showing the first signs of political consciousness that would shortly develop into the Mau-Mau movement.

Bishop Heffernan returned to Nairobi on the 28 November. Two days later he and Edel had a three-hour meeting. She was very satisfied with the outcome. 'The Bishop told me I had absolute freedom to do what I like and organise etc. They were there to fall in with whatever I arranged, and he had spoken of the Legion to his priests and given them to understand I had carte blanche and they were to afford me all the help possible.'

It all sounded as if Edel had nothing to do except push an open door. But her experience of extension work in England and Ireland had taught her differently. She knew she could do nothing without the permission of the bishop of the area, but she also knew that this permission was of no avail without the consent of the local parish priest or mission superior. Her task in Africa would be to travel around the various vicariates and prefectures, which corresponded to dioceses in countries where the Church was longer established. She had first of all to convince the bishop or prefect in charge that the Legion would help to build up the Church in his area. Having obtained his approval, she then had to go from one mission to another and sell the idea of the Legion to each individual superior.

The word 'sell' suggests that her role was like that of a commercial traveller. The comparison is not entirely far-fetched. She would have to visit people she did not know in places she did not know, giving them her sales-talk, answering their questions, meeting their objections, accepting rebuffs, keeping her good humour, persuading them that they needed the product she had on offer. She had done it at home. She could do it in Africa as well.

A salesman's strongest card is his faith in his product. This was something that Edel possessed in abundance. The reigning Pope, Pius XI, had from the beginning of his pontificate insisted on the need for what he termed Catholic Action. In his first encyclical letter, *Ubi Arcano* , issued in 1922, he called for the laity to take their full part in the mission of the Church. The work of proclaiming the Gospel was not to be confined to priests and religious. In many subsequent letters and addresses, he repeated the same message. Every Christian had the right and the duty to be an apostle.

The Legion of Mary, founded shortly before the accession of Pius XI, grew and developed in complete sympathy with his teaching. The first edition of the Handbook of the Legion of Mary was published in 1928 and was full of quotations from the writings of the Pope. The Handbook was the work of Frank Duff, though no author's name was given. It combined an account of the theology of the lay apostolate with a detailed description of the working of the Legion. The Handbook was every Legionary's *vade-mecum*. Edel's large travelling trunk was filled with copies. Every bishop or mission superior she visited was given one. It was her visiting card and her sales prospectus.

The Handbook went through several editions, each one longer than its predecessor. The Handbook that Edel brought with her in 1936 had 164 pages. (A new edition the following year had 291.) It opens with a description of the nature and object of the Legion.

Then comes a section on the devotional outlook of the Legion, which owes much to the writings of St Louis Marie de Montfort.

Under God, the Legion is built upon devotion to Mary, 'that ineffable miracle of the Most High' (Pius IX). Its trust in her is limitless, knowing that by the ordinance of God her power is without limit. All that He could give to Mary, He has given to her. All that she was capable of receiving, she has received in plenitude. For us God has constituted her a special means of grace. Operating in union with her we approach Him more effectively and hence win grace more freely. Indeed we place ourselves in the very floodtide of grace, for she is the spouse of the Holy Spirit; she is the channel of every grace which Jesus Christ has won. We receive nothing which we do not owe to a positive intervention on her part.

The book then moves on to questions of organisation. An interesting section entitled 'Objections Which May Be Anticipated' deals with a long list of arguments, the kind that Edel had already met in her extension work and would continue to meet for the rest of her life.

'The people are all good. We have flourishing Sodalities. We have no problems. The Priests and the Nuns are able to cope with the work.'

Even if there were no tragic self-deception at work here, there is another consideration as important as that of coping with the work. On all superiors rests responsibility for the bringing out to the full of the spiritual capacity of those in their charge. For the majority, this will be met by urging the performance of the essential duties or the frequent reception of the Sacraments. But in every flock a proportion will have the capacity to lead the apostolic life; and surely to leave that capacity undeveloped – hidden in the earth, as it were, like the talent in the Gospel – is a most serious default.

There follows a long description of the structure of the Legion. A legion (*legio* in Latin) was originally a regiment in the army of ancient Rome. Developing this theme, Frank Duff scoured his Latin dictionary for other military terms. As the language of the Church, Latin had an international dimension and this meant that new words did not have to be found in the native language of each new country where the Legion was set up.

The fundamental unit of the *Legio Mariae* (Legion of Mary) was the Praesidium, a group of members meeting once a week to pray and undertake apostolic work. When a number of Praesidia had been set up, a Curia was formed to supervise and coordinate their activity. Higher still was the Senatus, whose function was to oversee all the work of the Legion in an entire country or other large area. The supreme ruling body was the Concilium, which met every month in Dublin and regulated Legion activity throughout the world.

Other Latin terms used were *vexillum*, *acies* and *tessera*. The *vexillum* was the standard carried into battle by each Roman legion. The name was applied to the Legion standard, which was placed on the table at every Praesidium meeting. A larger version formed the centre-piece at the *Acies* (the Roman battle-line), which was an annual rally of the Praesidia in each Curia's area. The *tessera*, originally a small tablet giving the password for entering a Roman army camp, was the Legion prayer-card. It was a small four-page leaflet, which had a striking coloured picture on the front depicting Mary as Queen of the Legion. The remaining three pages gave the Legion prayers which were recited publicly at all meetings and privately by each member every day.

One point hammered home again and again by the Handbook was that the Legion system was invariable. Suggestions that the prayers were too long or the meetings too frequent or the work obligation too burdensome were not to be entertained.

The Legion notifies its members that they are not at liberty to vary rules and practices as they choose. The system prescribed is the Legion system. Each variation, however slight, makes others inevitable, till presently a body is in existence which indeed bears the name but possesses little else of the Legion, and which the Legion if made aware of the facts would not hesitate to disown, even though work in itself valuable is being done.

This inflexibility was one of the Legion's most striking characteristics. It was run as a benevolent dictatorship and Frank Duff's word was law. This was one of the reasons for its success. The carefully planned structure ensured effective action. The Legionary reported to the Praesidium, the Praesidium to the Curia, the Curia to the Senatus, the Senatus to the Concilium. Any weak points could be quickly spotted and attended to. Opponents of the Legion criticised it for its almost military discipline. Frank Duff took this criticism as a compliment. The Legion was, as its name suggested, an army; and military discipline was exactly what an army needed if it was to achieve its objectives.

This was the package which Edel was about to offer to the missionaries of East Africa. She knew they would give it a mixed reception. Some would be hostile to the Legion, seeing it as an alien import, untried in Africa and unsuited to its needs. Some would be wearily indifferent, worn out by years of strenuous labour and scant results and suspicious of instant solutions to perennial problems. Some would welcome it with open arms, sharing her vision of the Legion as the only effective way of making apostles out of ordinary men and women.

It would be her duty to win over the hostile, convince the waverers, and inspire the sympathetic. She was confident that with God's help she could do it. 'If a man only make a better mouse-trap than his neighbour,' said Emerson, 'the world will beat a path to his door.' Edel believed that the product she had to offer was the best there was.

ELEVEN

Nairobi Beginnings

Edel's first target was the parish priest of Nairobi. It was to be a baptism of fire. Bishop Heffernan had asked her to begin by setting up a Praesidium for Europeans and Goans. She had hoped to set up Praesidia involving all races but he told her that this was out of the question; indeed, it would be difficult enough to get Europeans and Goans to work together. Once this first Praesidium had been set up, she could see about starting Praesidia for Africans in the native missions.

The two principal Catholic churches in Nairobi were Holy Family and St Peter Claver's. Holy Family was the parish church, attended mainly by Europeans and Goans (known collectively as nonnatives). St Peter Claver's was called a mission church and was intended for natives. The Bishop told Edel to start by seeing the parish priest of the Church of the Holy Family, Father P. J. O'Flynn. Edel did not look forward to the meeting.

> This was a crux in one way, as the latter is not in too good health and consequently is not anxious to have anything new, or in fact anything that means a little extra work; he has a very nervous manner and is rather tactless and through no fault of his has managed to run up against most of his parishioners and others; his health is really the reason I believe. However, I saw him and of course, with the Bishop at the back, he agreed to think about it and discuss it with him. He suggested dealing with it some time after the New Year. I spoke about next week, which nearly finished him.

Despite the priest's obvious lack of enthusiasm, Edel pressed on with her plan. With the Bishop's support, she arranged to have a meeting in the parish hall on the evening of 8 December, the Feast of the Immaculate Conception. At the meeting she intended to give a talk on the Legion and ask for volunteers. She had never given a public speech before and the prospect filled her with dread. Her nervousness was not eased by the parish priest, who continued to put obstacles in her path right up to the last moment.

Just before the meeting the Parish Priest told me also that on page something of the Handbook it said that one must not start if there was not a reasonable chance of success. Just imagine having the Handbook quoted against you! He also told me to insist that first a work be decided upon, as he could not see any scope for work, and then ask if anyone would do it; a bit illogical.

About twenty-five Europeans and Goans turned up for the meeting. Edel had prepared her talk very carefully and she felt it went off well. 'I rubbed in as requested the work and meeting obligation; and also rubbed in the need for organised Catholic action and the futility of the individual hoping to persevere on his own without any such organisation.' Then she asked for questions and volunteers.

The parish priest opened fire at once. He complained that they already had too many organisations and that they only led to incidents and trouble. He said he did all the work that had to be done and there was nothing anyone else could do. He was backed up by Kenya's leading lay Catholic, Sir Joseph Sheridan, who was Chief Justice of the country and reminded Edel of her Uncle Frank. His approach was much more gentle than the priest's but he was firm in his opinion that the Society of St Vincent de Paul was capable of dealing with any work that had to be done.

Edel began to feel completely isolated. The Bishop, on whose support she had been relying, had failed to turn up: he said afterwards he had forgotten. Night was falling rapidly and the darkness in the room was in keeping with her feelings. Then someone produced a seven-branched candlestick from the church and lit it. Suddenly the tide began to turn. Help came unexpectedly from two of her friends. One was Jack Byrne, who with his wife Nancy had befriended her since her arrival in Nairobi. The other was Elizabeth

Gannon, whom she had met on the *Llangibby* and noted in her log
'would be good in Legion, I think'.

> Miss Gannon, who was out on the boat with me, brought the mat-
> ter to a head by stating that she could produce alone from her
> neighbourhood 14 children who needed Catechism instruction
> and had not got it, this amongst the people attending secondary
> schools here. This point was debated and immediately it was de-
> cided that if such was the case, a trial should be given. Sir Joseph
> said he had no idea such was the case.
>
> So volunteers were again asked for. Nine offered, three men
> and six women. Of the latter, two are coloured (I do not think
> they are Goans, no one is quite sure!) Then again the Parish Priest
> etc. called for a women's branch for a start, so perforce we had to
> fall in. Finally, Sir Joseph said if the women's succeeded and a
> men's were formed, he was quite willing to join the latter, and
> now would be an auxiliary member. He also offered on behalf of
> the V. de Paul to help in any way and suggested that they might
> arrange to give the children a lift if the distance question entered
> in too largely.

The inaugural meeting of the new Praesidium was arranged for
the following Tuesday at 5.30 p.m. Edel returned to the convent
drained by the ordeal but elated by the result. It had not been a complete victory. The Praesidium was smaller and more narrowly based
than she had hoped for. It consisted of four Irish women, including
Elizabeth Gannon and her sister, Mrs Máiréad O'Shea, and two
Goans, also sisters. There were no men, because of the parish
priest's veto. But the wonder was that it had come into being at all.

> I must say that no other Praesidium could ever again possibly
> have as much opposition in this country. It did not worry me un-
> duly as I know so many branches abroad have flourished though
> opposed at first. However, here there was the colour question, the
> prejudice of Indians having their homes visited, transport, and the
> objections raised by well-meaning people who had experience of

the country, which I had not. So if there is failure, the blame is mine; my only plea is that there is work to be done, the impossible has happened in other places, and one has to make a bit of allowance for grace and faith.

The throwaway reference in the last line is very typical of Edel. She was never one to parade her spirituality in her talk or writing. 'One has to make a bit of allowance for grace and faith' was as far as she was willing to go in revealing the prayer and trust that lay behind her every action.

Things went much more smoothly in the native mission. The priest in charge at St Peter Claver's was a man in his early thirties, Father Tom Maher. He had been among the welcoming party at the railway station when Edel and the Loreto nuns arrived in Nairobi. His attitude was very different from Father O'Flynn's. He welcomed Edel and the Legion unreservedly, becoming and remaining one of her staunchest supporters all during her time in East Africa.

He invited her to come to the Church for Mass on Sunday 13 December and afterwards to address a meeting in the nearby school. Her reception was in marked contrast to what happened at Holy Family. A car arrived to collect her at the convent at 6.30 a.m. When she got to the church the 7 a.m. Mass was just beginning. She was told that special arrangements had been made for her to receive Communion at a side altar so that she would not have to fast too long. After she had received, she found herself installed on a kneeler at the front of the crowded church to her considerable embarrassment. Eventually the priest came to rescue her and bring her to his house for a cup of tea. There he told her that the next Mass at 8 a.m. was a High Mass in honour of the Feast of the Immaculate Conception and would be offered for the success of the new Praesidium. 'Now was not that an absolutely perfect start to the Legion among the natives in East Africa?' she wrote to a friend. 'He is a very zealous priest and also a very practical and shrewd one; and many other priests call at his mission and if it goes well there it should be a centre for radiation.'

The meeting itself took place after the Mass and did not disappoint her. When Father Maher brought her in, she found the room decked with flowers and a statue of Our Lady in the place of honour. About a hundred people were waiting to hear her, all Africans.

They all clapped when I went in!! The meeting was very business-like; they had to be given a detailed account of the Legion, origin and all, though I had anticipated that a simpler account would have done; and on the priest's advice I mentioned the approbation of Mgr Riberi and the Bishop as an introduction. In actual fact they got exactly the same information as the non-native branch and asked actually more intelligent questions, from the point of view of accepting that the Legion was workable, and inquiring how binding the meeting obligation was in case of sickness and transfer; they also inquired what happened if they had to go to the Reserve (i.e. back to tribe) and no meeting was available etc.

Anyway, the whole initial talk and their discussion – about 8 of them got up with queries like the above – lasted well over an hour; the priest interpreted and gave a short exhortation. After all this, we retired for about 10 minutes whilst they considered it all. On our return we got 16 men, three women, and eight women from the school.

It was arranged that the new Praesidium would meet at 9.30 a.m. on the following Sunday, 20 December. Edel discovered that for most Africans the only practicable day for a meeting was Sunday. Their work kept them busy during the daylight hours on weekdays and they did not like going too far from their homes once night had fallen. She could see that as the number of African Praesidia increased her Sundays would become more and more crowded. Even at this stage it was clear that, with 16 men and 11 women already committed and others expressing interest, there would soon be three or more Praesidia attached to St Peter Claver's mission. It was a problem, but a happy one.

In the meantime the non-native Praesidium was finding its feet. Edel appointed her shipmate Elizabeth Gannon as its president. Two of the Goans were secretary and treasurer. Others began to join, both European and Asian. Within the meeting she found little in the way of racial tension. Outside the meeting she was still capable of being hurt by the discrimination that ran all through Kenyan society.

To give you an idea of the Colour question here, I arranged to meet the Goan treasurer on a certain day down town with a view to telling her her duties and explaining several things, and there was not a cafe or place I could take her to where she would not have been asked to leave. The only solution, when having an officers' meeting to go into various points when the school was not available, was to go to a hotel, the proprietor being known to the President, and privately explain the difficulty, and as a great favour he gave us his private office at the top of the building!

The only slight drawback was the spiritual director. In spite of his doubts about the Legion – or perhaps because of them – Father O'Flynn had decided to act as the Praesidium's director. He still could not see any need for the Legion or any work for it to do and he exuded pessimism all over the meetings. 'The advice I get all round is "Don't mind James" – that is from the clergy! I explained his nerves are bad.'

The first meeting of the native Praesidium at St Peter Claver's was held as planned and was full of promise for the future. The only problem was the language difficulty. The members belonged to different tribes and spoke different tribal languages. None of them could speak English with any ease but most of them knew some Swahili and so the meeting was conducted in Swahili. The priest had to translate everything they said for Edel and everything she said for them, which greatly lengthened the proceedings. 'I am going to have a shot at getting a smattering of Swahili,' she promised, 'it is not impossible. Apparently by application, given time, it can be done in six months.' In spite of her resolve, she never became fluent in the language. There were always so many other things to be done, and as her work expanded it brought her into areas where even Swahili was not understood.

With the approach of Christmas, she abandoned her plans to visit missions outside Nairobi until the new year. This did not prevent her from making contacts with the priests in charge of some of these missions and lining them up for attention in January and February. She made arrangements to have the Legion prayers translated into Swahili and printed and she renewed her resolution to learn the language herself. Then she sensibly decided to relax a little for the few days of Christmas.

She managed to fit in a few games of tennis. She found that the only suitable time was between 5 and 6 p.m., when the heat of the day had died down and night had not yet fallen. She attended to her rather basic wardrobe: 'an Irish woman here is altering the skirt of my costume, it was too wide, she offered to do it, and also to run me up a frock if I wanted it. Isn't that decent? I am often with them for tea or supper, etc.' She enjoyed the hospitality of her Irish friends, the Byrnes and the O'Sheas, and went to the pictures to see *Mutiny on the Bounty* , which she enjoyed greatly.

She was returning from one of these social evenings when she found herself unexpectedly confronted with the world she had left behind. She described it in a letter to her family.

On Friday night we listened in at the Convent at 12.30 midnight to the King's speech of abdication and allegiance to the Duke of York. Most of the nuns, and the priest who had lent and was manipulating the wireless, sat and talked from 10 p.m. on till it came through. We had coffee to keep us awake. I assure you I would never have stayed up but had been out to dinner to some Irish people and came in at 9.30 p.m. and walked into the gathering, so had to stay more or less.

She may have exaggerated her lack of interest a little. It was not the done thing in 1936 for Irish people to show too much concern about the English monarchy. But the fascination with the royal soap opera crossed all frontiers. The live broadcast of Edward VIII's abdication speech was possibly the first occasion when the whole world could listen in and hear history as it was being made.

The crowning touch came when a jackal emerged from the darkness on to the steps of the convent and howled mournfully all during the King's speech.

TWELVE

The First Acies

The beginning of 1937 saw the beginning of Edel's travels in East Africa. During the next three years she was to journey all over the four countries in the region that were under British control: Kenya, Uganda, Tanganyika and Zanzibar. Nairobi remained her headquarters but as her net widened her absences grow more frequent and prolonged. For weeks and even months on end she journeyed from one mission to another, with a suitcase in which her few clothes jostled for space with the Legion handbooks. Everywhere she went she was accompanied by the invaluable Baby Empire, so that she could keep up with her vast and ever increasing correspondence. She often brought a camera as well to take pictures for Legion publicity, but her photographs had an unfortunate habit of not turning out.

Her health held up remarkably well under extremely testing conditions. She kept pushing herself to the limit not out of recklessness but because she felt her time was short and she must use every minute. She had occasional illnesses but they were no more than what any white newcomer to Africa must expect. Many of those who met her were quite unaware that she was living under a sentence of death. Only the occasional bout of coughing suggested that all was not well.

She began with the missions within easy reach of Nairobi. On the afternoon of Sunday 3 January she went to Kiambu. She had been at St Peter Claver's that morning for the meeting of the native Praesidium. All was going well there, the number of members was increasing, the work was being done. 'You will be glad to hear,' she told Frank Duff, 'that one of the women, whose work was visitation of the native hospital, was able to baptize two persons, a woman and a baby and both died. This is the first direct fruit, though of course a few had been brought in to be taught Catechism to, and some careless persons reminded of their duties, so naturally it was an encouragement to the Legionaries.' After the meeting at St Peter Claver's she travelled the twelve miles or so to Kiambu, to meet the congregation after the afternoon Benediction.

The Mission, which consists of school, church and priest's house, is built on a hill between two bigger hills, if you can imagine that; a hill in a hollow, I heard it described as. Well, of course, by now I suppose you realise that any kind of European not a nun or a priest doing any Church work is a 'sight'. The congregation turned out, very colourfully dressed, sizes and ages ranging from kiddies of four and five to the oldest Christian who has 40 years to his credit! The Father in charge, Father Lynch, moved me off to the school, but the sightseers and hearers would not all fit, so it had to be an open-air business. These people were mostly Kikuyus and, as I mentioned, are intelligent and politically minded; they are of a light brown, almost a toast colour.

Anyway, I started with a chair for support, with Father Lynch on one side and the teacher, who was acting as interpreter, on the other. The teacher in this case knew English, as long as it was not too 'awkwardly' put; and I gave him just a sentence or two at a time and he conveyed the meaning to them. Father Lynch explained a little more in Swahili. Anyway, it wound up in their deciding they would like time to think it over as they had nothing like it before and so they are to get a week till next Sunday after Mass, when those who want to join are to turn up. Father Lynch, whom I met today, said several intend joining; he intends to have a mixed Praesidium. He says the news of it spread like wildfire from last Sunday's meeting.

It was a curious sensation to explain it to such a crowd, people all round one and the kiddies in front; and as a background, about six or seven pagan women, with ear decorations, who were passing that way, who listened in and then slipped off after the talk. Then the questions, the few they were, were given in a bantering sort of way, it was all a goodhumoured sort of business. Apparently you cannot rush the Kikuyus! However, I will tell you what transpires after next Sunday morning.

The following Sunday saw her back in Kiambu at 8.15 a.m. Seven men and three women had decided to join and the first meeting of the new Praesidium was held. Officers were elected and work was assigned. The work included looking after the careless, visiting the hospital, preparing people for baptism, and inquiring about children who were absent from school. 'It seems that every Kikuyu family, when asked how many children they have, say 'Two, one minding the flocks, the other at school' and unless one knows to the contrary they would get away with it. The extras in fact are all on the flock-minding.'

There were half a dozen other missions in the area where the priests were showing interest and where she hoped to be able to set up Praesidia before long. Things looked so hopeful that by the middle of January she was telling Bishop Heffernan of her plans to hold an Acies in March, the ceremony during which the members of the different Praesidia would meet together and re-affirm their commitment to the Legion. She hoped to have it on or about 25 March, the Feast of the Annunciation. She asked the bishop if it could be 'an all-colour Acies'. Even if the Praesidia were racially segregated, she felt that they could all meet on an equal footing to declare their common commitment. The bishop was doubtful if it could be done. 'The matter is left in abeyance for the moment,' she wrote. 'I will have it out with him again.'

She had to admit that he had grounds for doubt. She was trying to start a junior Praesidium in the school attached to the Loreto Convent where she was staying, but the colour question was frustrating her plans. There were no African pupils in the school, but there were a number of Goans and Seychellois and these were looked down on by the white girls.

For the proposed junior Praesidium we had a few prospective whites, two Goan girls and one Seychellois girl. The latter had on her own initiative rounded up some children for the instruction classes when she heard them announced in Church, and when I explained the Legion to the Children of Mary attached to her school, had volunteered to join. Well, when we were discussing the formation of the junior Praesidium, it was brought up that the Seychellois were not very 'mixable' with the whites, they were inclined to be 'cheeky', to 'recognise them outside meetings', and the whites would have the name of knowing 'that crowd.' Catholic action! It would really make you see red.

She never found it easy to identify with the white Kenyans. She was repelled by their brittle and selfish life-style and their disdain towards those they considered to be socially inferior, including other whites. The Catholics especially disappointed her. She felt that the bad example they gave was a hindrance to the work of the missionaries. She went to the Sundowner Dance, a social evening organised by the local Catholic Association on 23 January, and was distinctly unimpressed.

The Bishop and all the local clergy were at it, but from the point of view of bringing all the Catholics together it was not a success as there were only about 50 there. The trouble apparently is the question of class distinction, which appears to block anything out here. The first class officials won't go because the third class government officials may be there, and the majority of the latter won't go because they know they will be ignored by the former, a sort of circle.

Her judgement of the white Kenyans, based on only two months' acquaintance, might be considered a hasty one. But the passing of time did nothing to soften it. She grew more and more disenchanted with the mixture of snobbery, infidelity, drinks and drugs that characterised much of white society. A year later, writing to an Irish friend, she described it in a few bleak words. 'Did I ever tell you that the general phrase which perfectly sums up European life out here is: "Are you married or do you live in Kenya?" Every family you meet nearly or come in contact with bears it out. Of course, I suppose one always gets a lot of riff-raff in these colonies.'

She felt far more at home with Africans. 'Dealing with natives,' she wrote, 'is child's play compared to handling the non-natives.' Her next two targets were the native missions of Mangu and Kalimoni. Father Maher offered to drive her to Mangu, spend the day there, and then bring her on to Kalimoni, where he would leave her for the weekend. It did not work out exactly as planned. When she got to Mangu, she found a letter there from the priest in Kalimoni saying they had an outbreak of meningitis and she would have to postpone her visit. To make matters worse, the priest in Mangu was unwilling to start the Legion because there was a lot of anti-European feeling among the local Kikuyu people. However, Edel was not one to give in easily and she had an ally in her driver. 'Father Maher was very helpful as, knowing the ground, he was able to meet objections, and also was a friend of the priest, and thirdly gave results from his own Praesidium.' In the end, the priest agreed to start a Praesidium quietly, without making any public announcement. He would also consider the possibility of a junior Praesidium.

A few days later she went to Kabaa and spent the week-end there. There was a college and seminary in Kabaa with over a hundred African boys on the rolls. There was no difficulty in finding volunteers for a junior Praesidium and one of the priests on the staff agreed to look after it. On the Sunday morning she travelled ten miles to Kombe, an out-mission served from Kabaa, and attended Mass in the school. 'The school was simply made of planks, the walls only came up half way all round, so that those who could not fit in attended Mass from the outside. I knelt on a line with the little Mass altar box, on a sack, as the place was packed.'

After Mass she held the now customary meeting to explain the Legion. The people belonged to the Kamba tribe and everything she said had to be translated into their language. 'The Legion work here would be to baptize pagans in danger of death, visiting the sick, getting children to school, looking after many who have got careless or who have got too old to travel to the Mass centre, to ensure the sacraments to the dying.' She was pleased when twenty of the congregation gave in their names.

> The priest stayed a little to ask them about other matters and a number came outside and surrounded me. One of the teachers had a little English (he was trained at Kabaa) and they put me through my paces! Where was I from? Did I know were there any other priests coming out? What of the war in Spain? Would I come again? Thanks for coming! When I said I could not stay permanently with them as I did not know Kamba, he (acting as interpreter) started a great clap. I nearly faded away and said, 'What did you say?' 'The people are all very pleased, Mother, that you are going to learn Kamba,' was the reply!! The best moment was when he said, 'Mother, it is getting hot, you had better go into the car.' I assure you Mother went with a sigh of relief!

The first weekend of February was spent in Limuru. In addition to the church, school and priest's house, Limuru had a small convent of Loreto sisters, where Edel would often stay in times to come. The priest in charge was strongly in favour of the Legion and had already spoken to his congregation about it. As the people belonged to two different tribes, he had to use two different languages, Kikuyu for the Kikuyus and Swahili for the Kavirondos. After the second Mass on Sunday morning, an open-air meeting was held to launch the new Praesidium. Edel's report on the meeting captures much of the colour of the occasion.

> There was an obvious place in an opening shaded by trees, so a banner of Our Lady was nailed on to one tree on the edge of the circle to give the proper atmosphere. A small platform was brought out from the school on which was placed a table and a chair. The priest and I shared the platform.
>
> All round were gathered the men and women and the juniors, the men on the right and the women religiously on the left. (The Kikuyus have not much appreciation for the womenfolk, and the latter would not imagine it possible they could attend a meeting

at which the Lords of the flocks and herds were present. In fact, the women gathered at the far side of the church and the priest had to prevail upon them to join the general body of the meeting. He also told me to emphasise in my talk the part women played in the Legion, so as to educate the men to the fact that their wives could play a part in Legion activity.)

As usual, the women's group was colourful, in fact I doubt if a colour was missing, whilst the men were arrayed in the familiar motley garb ranging from precise European clothes to the poorest native dress, which consists of topcoat and soft hat with feather tucked in it.

The sacristan in long white robe with a small crucifix round his neck was in the front row, he is also cook to the mission, but the dignity his appearance lent to the scene was marred by the fact that he was inclined to doze. Be it noted he had been up since before 5 a.m. and between tolling the bell lustily at intervals, attending first Mass, seeing to the food for the nuns and mission, attending second Mass armed with a stick with which he poked and hit any children who fidgeted or crowded the benches, he earned a brief repose!

The priest in charge at Limuru, Father John Reidy, struck up an instant rapport with Edel and was to become one of her closest friends and supporters in Kenya. In addition to his enthusiasm for

Edel with Fr John Reidy.

the Legion, it turned out that he came from Co. Clare and knew many of her relations on her mother's side. One of the nuns in the convent felt some unease at the obviously good relationship between Edel and the priest, who was some eight years her senior. She wrote Edel a letter advising her to cut short her visit to Limuru as her friendship with Father Reidy was causing scandal to the Africans. It was a useful letter in that it showed Edel how careful she would have to be regarding her own reputation and the reputation of the priests she visited, but at the same time it must have been more than a little hurtful.

Each new mission contacted meant not just one visit but a whole series. There was a first visit to meet the priests and sisters. Then a second to address the Sunday congregation and ask for volunteers. The third was for the first meeting of the new Praesidium – or Praesidia if there was a junior one attached to the school. Further visits were often needed to sort out teething troubles and make sure that everything was running smoothly. By the middle of February she found she was spending only a couple of days a week in Nairobi. In a letter to her family written on Ash Wednesday, she apologised for not being able to answer all their letters immediately.

Yesterday I attended another meeting and had pancakes in the morning and was out to one family with a party for a sundowner, and then back to the Byrnes for a snack supper and we got home about 11.30 p.m. so we celebrated Shrove in style. Today I have another meeting, tomorrow I motor to start two junior branches at a place called Mangu; stay the night at a convent – there is nothing usually at these out-missions in Kenya but a mission and a convent, this is the French convent – get a lift in by lorry to a place Kalimoni, talk to the nuns and see how the land lies for a branch; am collected there and motored back to Nairobi, it is only 37 miles away. Motor the following day to Limuru for the weekend and another meeting. This is just to give you an idea of how the time goes. So I have not much time for writing this week.

In point of fact, she wrote very frequently to her family. These letters are naturally different from those written to Legion headquarters. None of her family were in the Legion, so she devotes little space to Legion news and avoids Legion terminology. Instead, she describes the people and the countryside and records her surprisingly rare glimpses of wild animals. She talks about her social life, probably exaggerating it a little in order to assure her mother that she was keeping well and not over-working. And she includes plenty of fashion notes for her three younger sisters, to prove that she has not relapsed into dowdiness. 'In case you think my clothes are bedraggled, I have to be always pretty well turned out.' For their benefit she describes the send-off at the railway station for the Byrnes, who were going home on leave.

I had on a very swish two-piece, I only wear it on special occasions, a mauve crepe de chine. Well one of the priests first chaffed me about the mauve creation: 'Miss Quinn attended attired in mauve or heliotrope crepe de chine!' We drove back from the station to Peter Claver's mission for afternoon tea, there were four priests or so there and the bishop. The latter started then to tease me about the Mauve Creation, and finally when driving me up to my meeting said I was stealing his colour, showing me his purple socks! We agreed they were not the same shade, and I told him my mauve set off his grey in great style. When I was finally getting out of the car, I told him I'd never have courage to wear the rigout again after all the remarks. He told me to be sure and do so, it was very becoming – what else could he say, as I told him.

In mid-March she received a letter from Mombasa. It was from Father Engelbert, the secretary of the Apostolic Delegation. He told her that Archbishop Riberi would like to have a report on her Legion experience in East Africa and especially on the work of the Legion in Bishop Heffernan's Vicariate. She heard also on the grapevine that Bishop Heffernan had received a similar request. She set to work on a detailed report and posted it off in early April. It included an interesting list of the fourteen Praesidia that had been founded in the four months since she came to Africa.

NATIVE		Tribe	Est.	Nos.
St Peter Claver's, Nairobi	Mixed Praesidium	Kavirondo	15.12.36	17
Eastleigh Convent, Nairobi	Girls' do.	Mixed	1.1.37	15
Kiambu Mission	Mixed do.	Kikuyu	10.1.37	10
Kabaa Training College	Boys' do.	Mixed	31.1.37	20
Kombe, near Kabaa	Mixed do.	Kamba	21.2.37	30
Kalimoni School	Girls' do.	Mixed	22.2.37	15
Mangu Mission	Mixed do.	Kikuyu	26.2.37	10
Mangu Mission	Boys' do.	Kikuyu	26.2.37	15
Kalimoni Mission	Mixed do.	Kavirondo	2.3.37	11
Limuru Mission	Mixed do.	Kavirondo	11.4.37	12
NON-NATIVE				
Holy Family Church, Nairobi	Mixed do.	Europeans/Goans	15.12.37	9
Parklands Church	Women's do.	Europeans/Goans	10.2.37	9
Loreto Convent	Girls' do.	Europeans	24.2.37	10
Holy Family Church, Nairobi	Mixed do.	Europeans etc.	12.3.37	16

She lists the work being done by the various Praesidia. It includes visiting hospitals, visiting lapsed and careless Catholics, bringing in and helping to instruct catechumens, visiting prisons, getting children to come to school, helping to teach in the schools, looking after young children, ministering to the sick, maintenance of churches, sacristies and cemeteries. 'The more one is in contact with the various missions,' she concludes, 'the more one sees the possibilities for the Legion and the help it can be to the already overworked missionary.'

The culmination of this first phase of her work was the Nairobi Acies. It was held in St Peter Claver's Church at 3 p.m. on Low Sunday, 4 April 1937. It was attended by the six Praesidia which were within walking distance, five from Nairobi and one from Kiambu. As Kiambu was twelve miles away this meant a total walk of twenty-four miles for those who did not manage to get lifts.

Edel had her wish in regard to the mixture of races. Native and non-native Praesidia took part on an equal footing, or at least on as equal a footing as was possible in the Nairobi of those days. When the six Praesidia took their places in the church, it somehow happened that the non-native ones were in front of the native ones. Still, the important thing was that they were all there. Edel had been quite nervous before the ceremony but had to admit afterwards that everything went without a hitch. The legion altar was set up at the sanctuary gates, with the statue of the Blessed Virgin, candles and flowers. Beside it was a large-size Vexillum, the Legion standard, specially carved in camphor wood and painted by one of the sisters. A native choir had been trained to sing the hymns in Latin, English and Sawhili. A large congregation filled the rest of the church and watched the proceedings with much interest.

The ceremony opened with a hymn in English. 'The native choir,' Edel noted with satisfaction, 'rendered the English one, "O Purest of Creatures", very well and very distinctly and the Junior natives joined in as well as the non-natives.' After the rosary and opening prayers, two sermons were preached, one in English and one in Swahili. Then the Legionaries came to the altar one by one, placed a hand on the Standard, and made their consecration by saying, 'I am all thine, my Queen, my Mother, and all that I have is thine' in English, Swahili or Kikuyu. After the closing prayers came Benediction of the Blessed Sacrament with the traditional Latin chants, and the Acies concluded with a rousing hymn in Swahili.

A group photograph was taken of all the Legionaries on the front steps of the church. It still survives. Most of the hundred or so Legionaries are standing but there are chairs in front for the V.I.P.s These are the seven priests who attended and Edel. She is smiling a smile of quiet and understandable satisfaction.

THIRTEEN

Sickness and Health

There were two other centres of missionary activity in Bishop Heffernan's Vicariate of Zanzibar. One was the coastal strip around the port of Mombasa on the edge of the Indian Ocean. The other was the island of Zanzibar itself, which gave its name to the whole Vicariate. These were the next two items on Edel's agenda. She hoped to start in Mombasa before the end of May 1937.

Before she left Nairobi, she spent some time visiting the various Praesidia to make sure they were rooted and flourishing. There was always a gap between promise and fulfilment. The first flush of enthusiasm could fade very quickly, among priests as well as people. Indeed, a large proportion of her difficulties were with priests.

In writing to her family and friends, Edel always spoke of priests with the utmost charity and respect. Her confidential reports to the Legion headquarters were a different matter. In explaining why some Praesidia fell by the wayside, she had to give the causes and sometimes she had to admit that opposition or neglect on the part of the priest was a major factor. The rapid collapse of the Legion in Kalimoni was a case in point.

He admits that in the few weeks he had it, it did good work and brought him in numbers for Easter to the sacraments, but he is not prepared to go to the meetings; and though the members turned up, he did not go, so naturally the Praesidium could not go on. I mean you cannot expect natives to be inspired how to work on Legion lines unless they have someone to interpret the handbook and teach them, at least for the first few months. I told him of course that if they were helped for the first while, afterwards they could carry on themselves, provided he kept an eye on them. It amounts though to the fact that he was not prepared to go to the meetings at all, and that finished it. The priests here, many of them say that he is like that, wildly keen for three weeks and then as quickly changing to something else. The cruel part I see is that there is ample work waiting to be done and people ready to do it, and yet they are not even given a fair chance.

It is rarely that she speaks as openly as this. More often one has to read between the lines to sense the many disappointments and frustrations that came her way. In one of her letters around this time she answers a query from headquarters about a South African woman who was being considered for the work of Legion envoy in West Africa.

Re the remarks re rubbing people the wrong way and not getting on well with Irish priests: if the latter fact is true, from my little experience since I came out here I would say better have no-one there, than a person who is likely to do that. First, I think that the climate, life and work out here, which would apply much more in the West which is not so congenial, is apt to make people jumpy and easily put on edge. The priests themselves admit it here that after a few years out here no-one is quite normal, i.e. that they are inclined to be jumpy and act quickly, when if they thought a second time they would often act differently. This may sound ridiculous and I know I have put it badly, but it does not alter the fact. So that if you make a bad approach sometimes you might close a door.

One can only guess at the number of jumpy priests she had met and the number she was yet to meet during the course of her travels. If the testimony of those who knew her is to be believed, she herself even on her worst days was remarkable for her tact and patience. No door was ever closed through her fault.

She finally arrived in Mombasa on 29 May 1937. It was her first time there since she had landed and spent a few brief hours in the town six months previously. She was met by Father Lawless, whom she had known in Nairobi, and he brought her to the Loreto Convent, where she was to stay as the guest of the sisters. 'It is exceptionally kind of them here, because it is a new foundation and is naturally not overburdened with money.' The coastal heat was very oppressive, even though it was supposed to be the cool season. 'I have a huge room to myself, with glass all the way round and windows that open; at night several windows and the door are wide open; over the bed is the mosquito net, for there are some mosquitoes here and, whilst they are not bad, still their bite causes wee lumps like hives that are very irritating.'

One of her first visits was to the Apostolic Delegation, where Father Engelbert entertained her to morning tea. He told her that Archbishop Riberi was still on his visitation of the missions in West Africa but that he had received the reports from herself and Bishop Heffernan. There was no news of the letter that the Archbishop was to write to all the bishops about the Legion of Mary, but Father Engelbert believed that it would soon be on its way.

Her work in Mombasa followed the pattern already established in Nairobi. She visited missions in the town and outlying areas, met priests, addressed meetings, asked for volunteers, established Praesidia. She made little headway with the whites: there were only about fifty European Catholics in the town and not more than fifteen of them practised their religion. There was a sizeable Goan population and Africans of many different tribes and these offered a better opportunity. The diary she was keeping at the time has lists of meeting and appointments for the first two weeks in Mombasa which show that she was working as hard as ever. A letter written to John Nagle on 10 June assured him that an alarmist report about her health was without foundation.

Three days later came disaster. Her diary entry for Sunday 13 June 1937 records two events, a lecture and a Junior Praesidium meeting. Then comes a final entry which reads, 'Temp. 105 – 103.2 – 101.' By Sunday night she was evidently in the grip of a raging fever, checking her temperature anxiously from hour to hour and recording its rise and fall.

It was a crisis, but she saw it more as a crisis for her work than for herself. She was only six months in Africa and in a sense still on probation. If word got back to Dublin, her family would panic, her friends would start to agitate, and there would be severe pressure on Frank Duff to order her home with her work barely begun. She decided that no word of her illness must reach Ireland. But she was a public figure in constant touch with Irish missionaries, all writing home regularly. How could she keep her illness secret?

Sick though she was, she was still able to mastermind an extraordinary cloak-and-dagger operation. She sent a telegram to her most trusted ally, Father John Reidy of Limuru, telling him that she was taking the overnight train to Nairobi on Monday evening and asking him to meet her at Athi River. The plan worked perfectly. Father Reidy left Limuru early on Tuesday morning, collected Father Maher in Nairobi, and then went on to Athi River, about half an hour's drive from Nairobi. There they collected a very sick Edel from the train and brought her straight to Limuru, where she was at once given medical attention and put to bed in the Loreto sisters' convent. Her brief diary entry for the day reads, 'Met at Athi River – Limuru – Doc H – injection.' She does not give a name to her illness: it appears to have been a severe attack of malaria.

There are six blank pages for the next six days. The diary resumes on Tuesday 22 June with four brief words, 'Up for an hour.' Two days later she was up for all her meals. On Sunday 27 June she was able to attend a Curia meeting in Limuru and to resume her correspondence as if nothing had happened. The crisis was over and, astonishingly, not a word about it reached Ireland.

During her days of convalescence in Limuru, Father Reidy organised a treat in the form of a picnic for her and some of the sisters. They brought a camera along and took a number of photographs, one of Edel by herself, sitting on a rock against a background of flowering bushes and trees. The rest cure had evidently been a great success. She looks healthy and happy, her posture is relaxed, her face shows no sign of strain, and she has on her lips that charming and mischievous half-smile that her Irish friends knew so well. In a moment of inspiration, she had copies made of the photo and sent back to Dublin where they allayed any worries caused by the break in her correspondence. Her mother was so taken by it that she wrote back, 'The next thing we hear is you'll be getting married in Africa!'

She remained on for some weeks, first in Limuru, then in Nairobi, writing letters and attending occasional meetings. She did not leave until the evening of 23 July, arriving in the heat and humidity of Mombasa the following morning. Her diary entry begins, 'Got H.C. D.G.' She had eaten nothing on the train since midnight so that she could receive Communion on her arrival. Church law at the time required that anyone receiving Communion should fast from food and drink, including water, from midnight.

She resumed her work and succeeded in establishing Praesidia in all but one of the missions in the Mombasa area. The reason for the exception is interesting. Frank Duff had expressed some concern at the thought of woman envoys travelling on their own in the remoter parts of Africa. She assured him that there was no danger, as white women were treated in great respect by the natives. There was only

Edel in Limuru, at a picnic organised by Fr Reidy.

one problem. 'The whole crux would appear to be the "convent" one, I should say. There is one mission here, the furthest one out, where there is no convent. I haven't been to it, one would have to spend a few days.' She knew by now that the African Catholics were not used to the idea of a woman missionary who was not a nun. It would not be fitting for her to stay at a mission where the only accommodation was the priest's house.

She was still in Mombasa when she received a copy of the long-awaited letter from Archbishop Riberi. Dated 25 June 1937, it was sent to every one of the thirty-three ordinaries (heads of Vicariates and Prefectures) for whom he was responsible. It was all she could have asked for and a good deal more.

The Delegate began his lengthy letter with a history of the Legion of Mary and a description of the kind of work it did. He stressed also the spiritual and moral formation which the members themselves received from their meetings. He went on to speak about the Pope's call for Catholic Action and strongly recommended the Legion as a suitable response: 'I like to think that it is the nearest approach to the ideal of Catholic Action as fostered by the Holy Father.' The last part of the letter dealt specifically with Edel and her work.

Last summer the Concilium Legionis, which has its headquarters in Dublin, decided, at the special request of Mgr Heffernan, Vicar Apostolic of Zanzibar, to send a propagandist to his Vicariate, in the person of Miss Edel Quinn. I was requested to give her a letter of recommendation and introduction to the Ordinaries of East Africa. While warmly encouraging the initiative of going to Kenya, I delayed the giving of such recommendation until I myself had acquired a better knowledge of the working of the Legion in missionary countries. This I have been able to see in West Africa, where I came into direct contact with the Legion's successful work.

I am able to state now that the Ordinaries of the Gold Coast and those of Nigeria have, at their last conference, adopted the Legion of Mary as the means of developing Catholic Action.

Meanwhile I have received from His Lordship Bishop Heffernan a report of the working of the Legion in his Vicariate. What he tells me is most encouraging.

The time has come, therefore, for me to give Miss Quinn the desired recommendation and introduction. Hence, my recommendation is an earnest one. I understand that Miss Quinn, who is still working in Zanzibar Vicariate, is willing and ready to lend her organising activities wherever they will be requested. If you desire further information about her work, please write to Mgr Heffernan, Nairobi. I may point out that all her expenses are covered by the headquarters of the Legion.

Meanwhile I shall request Miss Quinn to send you a copy of the Handbook of the Legion to supplement the scanty information about the Legion contained in this letter.

As soon as she had seen the letter, Edel hurried over to the Delegation to see Father Engelbert and to get the names and addresses of the prelates to whom she was to send the Handbook. He suggested that she should wait until the new edition of the Handbook arrived as, unlike the previous edition, it had an *Imprimatur*. She wrote at once to Dublin asking for a consignment of the new Handbooks to be sent out, making no attempt to conceal her delight.

Father E. told me he was surprised at the warmth of the Delegate's letter, that it was much more than an ordinary letter of recommendation and even its very length was unusual. That from him meant a lot, because he is not usually expansive. He also said he had recently one or two inquiries from bishops as regards the best system of Catholic Action or rather asking for his suggestions, and he had told them of the Legion. There are 33 Ordinaries and he was very tickled at the idea of getting them all in. He told me I would be an old lady by the time they were finished!!

Bishop Heffernan arrived in Mombasa towards the end of July and caused a change of plan. His next stop was Bura and he suggested that Edel go with him, as it was the only mainland part of his Vicariate she had not yet visited. Bura would be a good jumping off ground for the Vicariate of Kilimanjaro, which Edel had already been invited to visit by the Vicar, Bishop Joseph Byrne. She could postpone the island of Zanzibar until the new year.

Her last meeting in Mombasa was on Sunday 15 August. The next day she left for Bura. The convoy set out at 1.35 p.m. and consisted of two vehicles. Edel travelled in a car with the bishop and one of the priests. An African driver in a lorry took a second priest together with a heavy load of baggage and supplies. Edel's contribution was a case of clothes, a case of literature, a hatbox and a typewriter.

The journey of one hundred and twenty-five miles was her longest road journey so far. The road, primitive at the best of times, had been transformed into a sea of mud by a night of torrential rain. The bishop, who was driving, found it hard to control the car. It skidded several times and finally ended up embedded in the mud. It took the men half an hour to get it moving again. Soon after they had a chance to stop for tea. 'Tea included ham, chicken and egg sandwiches, biscuits, cake, tea, coffee and sweets! (Life in darkest Africa!)'

They resumed their journey and managed to negotiate a swollen river. Night was falling and they were about ten miles from their destination when they came across two white women and a car with a punctured tyre. 'Out all the men got again and after an hour they had the spare wheel changed for her. One of the dames was of uncertain age in white blouse and trousers and the car was a very ancient Ford and all the tyres were worn to the last. They were driving altogether over 200 miles on this particular trip.' It was 8 p.m. when they finally saw the lights of Bura and steamed up the hill to the welcome and warmth of the mission.

The two weeks she spent in Bura were something of a rest, at least according to the letters she sent to her family. Apart from the mission, there was just one out-station to be visited, which gave her leisure for reading and writing. She resumed her Swahili studies with the help of an English-speaking native from the school. 'As well as this, I can sit out all day in a deck chair under the trees, go for a walk up the hill in the evening, and get down some of my letter arrears; I have a good deal of writing to do now, with the local Praesidia and Curias started, as well as to home people.'

Almost from the beginning, her letters to her family and especially to her mother were written under a sense of strain. She had to project the image of being at all times in perfect physical and mental health. None of Mrs Quinn's letters survive but their tone can easily be gathered from Edel's replies. If there was the slightest reference to working hard, or travelling long distances, or feeling tired, Mrs Quinn would put the most pessimistic construction upon it. If there was any delay in the arrival of mail from Africa, she would assume that Edel was ill or dying and write agonised letters of concern and remonstrance. She could not understand how little time Edel had for writing home or how difficult it was to get letters posted from some of the remoter missions.

While this motherly concern was understandable and indeed praiseworthy, it had a depressing effect on Edel. She could not write home freely about her work or discuss honestly her state of health. It was not long before Mrs Quinn began to suspect this and to complain that she was not being told the full truth. It was a self-fulfilling complaint. The more she accused Edel of not telling the full facts, the more Edel was inclined to hide them. She no longer felt able to confide in her family and receive from them the kind of support that she needed. Mrs Quinn's motherly love was genuine and deeply felt; but it was the kind that smothers, not the kind that gives strength.

Edel's letter from Bura is a case in point. 'I can sit out all day in a deck chair under the trees' is strictly speaking true: she could if she wanted to. But it is the last thing she would ever dream of doing as long as she was physically capable of standing up. The same air of unreality hangs over Edel's description of the food she was being given in the convent, in response to her mother's suggestion that she might not be getting enough to eat.

Now for the menu which has varied every day since I came. Breakfast: porridge (now off the menu as left), rasher and two eggs, fruit local, bananas or paupau, bread and butter and tea; this is at 7.20 a.m. At 10 a.m. cocoa and homemade biscuits. Lunch at 12.10: soup, meat, two kinds of vegetables, tomatoes, salad, cabbage, spinach or some local vegetables, potatoes, sweet, coffee. Tea 3 p.m.: tea, bread and butter, fruit, bananas, biscuits or homemade cake. Dinner: same as lunch, only I have tea after it with biscuits or cake or pancakes or fritters!! On Friday it was tinned salmon! So now do not say I may not get food.

All these good things may indeed have been on the menu, but it is inconceivable that Edel could have changed the habits of a lifetime and eaten on such a gargantuan scale.

By the end of August she had finished her work in Bura, the last mission in the Vicariate of Zanzibar, apart from the island of Zanzibar itself. It was time to move on. The bishop and his car were gone, but Bura was on a railway line and was visited by a passenger train once a week. It came every Wednesday from Mombasa and went on to Moshi, her next destination. At 5.45 on the morning of 1 September she boarded the train at Bura station, having provided herself as usual with a second-class ticket. But the guardian angel who watched over all her travels was still at work and she found herself assigned to a first-class carriage for the six-hour journey.

FOURTEEN

Cows and Lions

At noon on 1 September 1937 Edel entered what was literally a new country. Tanganyika was a former German colony which had been mandated to Britain after the defeat of Germany in the First World War. It had a population of about five million, a million or so more than Kenya. It was poorer in resources than Kenya and with a less attractive climate, so it had drawn far fewer European settlers. In 1964, after it had gained independence, it joined with Zanzibar to form the present Tanzania.

During the course of her train journey from Bura Edel crossed the frontier and when she alighted at Moshi she had to go through the formalities of presenting her passport and having her baggage examined by customs. She found a taxi waiting for her at the station with orders from the bishop to take her to the Kilimanjaro Hotel. The drive gave her an opportunity to see her first Tanganyikan town. It was little different from any town in Kenya.

Moshi is a one-street town, two stores, three hotels small bungalow type, two banks, Barclay's and the Standard, and the Post Office. There is a chemist's shop attached to one of the stores. The latter are the kind you would imagine in an out-of-the-way Wild West Story, apples, oranges, frocks, writing materials, boot polish etc., and sweets all mixed up. Moshi is of recent growth, some 20/30 years back, when the railway came there.

In the hotel she had lunch with the Vicar Apostolic of Kilimanjaro, Bishop Joseph Byrne, and one of his priests, Father Albrecht, a native of Alsace. The Vicariate was now under the care of Holy Ghost Fathers from the American province, many of them with Irish ancestry and Irish names. Bishop Byrne was himself born in Ireland but had become a U.S. citizen. There were also a number of older priests who had come out during the German administration, mainly from Alsace.

After lunch Edel did some shopping in the town and went to the Post Office to arrange for a transfer of funds. She was paid an allowance of £50 a quarter by the Legion, which was supposed to cover all her expenses. In his letter to the bishops, Archbishop Riberi had emphasised the fact that she was financially independent and would not be a burden on any mission she visited. She always made an offering to cover her expenses of food and lodging. Sometimes the offer was declined, but not many missions were rich enough to afford such a gesture.

When she had finished her shopping, the Bishop drove her the twenty-five miles to the mission at Kilema, where she was to stay. The road led steadily uphill, winding around the foot of Mount Kilimanjaro, the highest mountain in Africa. They stopped for afternoon tea at the seminary, where there were nearly a hundred students preparing for the priesthood. Eight of them were close to ordination. Edel was intrigued by their dress, which combined a long soutane with bare feet. Then they continued on to Kilema, the Bishop's residence and the ecclesiastical capital of the Vicariate of Kilimanjaro. Edel was to stay in the convent with the Sisters of the Precious Blood, all of them from German-speaking countries but with a fair grasp of English.

There are about 7 or 8 nuns, one is in charge of the hospital which has 40 beds, she is also a dentist. They have a school of 60 boarders and 1300 odd daily scholars. They have five native nuns to help them. I have a large bedroom upstairs with a verandah on either side, one lounge chair, one large office table, and sitting room downstairs. I work mostly upstairs. The sight here is Kilimanjaro itself, which is 19,300 feet high. We are up over 4,000 here and snow begins from 12,000 feet up I believe. It has been shrouded in clouds for the last few days but I am on the lookout for a glimpse of it. I believe it is an exquisite sight in moonlight.

The sheer size of the mission impressed her greatly. She estimated that the church held between two and three thousand people.

It was packed for all three Masses on Sunday, one for married people, one for children and one for young unmarried people. She could not imagine how such large congregations could be drawn from so remote and desolate an area. Confessions were heard on three days a week: Thursday for children, Friday for women, Saturday for men. There were organisation to cater for all wants. There was a Conference of the St Vincent de Paul Society to help the needy. There were confraternities of St Anne and St Joseph for the married women and men respectively, the Children of Mary for the unmarried women, and the Sodality of St Aloysius for the unmarried men and boys. She began to wonder if they would feel any need for yet another organisation.

The Bishop soon dispelled her fears. He was in no doubt about the value of the Legion of Mary as a means of involving lay people in the work of evangelisation. He brought priests in from outside missions to meet Edel and hear about the Legion. He called groups of the more committed Christians together and urged them to join. With his approval and support Edel began the familiar round of consultations and meetings which had to pave the way for each new Praesidium.

Two of the nuns who were stationed at Kilema at the time, Sister Angelita and Sister Ignatius, gave evidence before the canonisation tribunal in Nairobi in 1966. They described the way Edel spent her day. She began with prayer. She was in the church every morning for the six o'clock Mass. The nuns invited her to join them but she preferred to kneel with the Africans on their rough and rather uncomfortable kneelers. After hearing Mass and receiving Holy Communion, she remained on in the church until about 7.30. Then she went to the convent for a quick breakfast. When the nuns were on their way to the school at 7.45 they could hear the sound of the Baby Empire from her room.

Her circle of correspondents was large and growing. Almost every week she wrote a lengthy report to the Legion headquarters in Dublin, addressed either to Brother Nagle or Mr Duff. She also sent them official notifications and registration forms for the various Praesidia and Curiae that were set up. There were equally long letters for her family, some addressed to 'My dear Family', others to 'My dearest Popa' or 'My darling Mums' or Leslie or Mona or Ralph or John. She kept in contact with her old friends in Ireland, especially her Legion friends. There were 'Dear Gang' letters, as well as letters to such friends as Emma Bodkin and Celia Shaw. Then there were letters to her new friends in Africa. She knew how important it was to keep in contact with the priests and sisters who had undertaken the spiritual direction of the various Legion groups. Every new Praesidium set up was a new correspondent to be written to.

She usually joined the sisters for a cup of tea at 10 a.m. Then she visited one of the missions in the neighbourhood. If it was not too far away, she went on foot. She describes one such expedition which she made in company with one of the sisters.

She was surprised to see that the apparently deserted countryside was in fact well populated, with native huts half hidden by the banana groves. She visited a homestead which consisted of two huts, one round and one rectangular. The family comprised husband, wife, children and mother-in-law, together with cows, calves, goats, hens and 'the most miserable specimen of a dog I ever saw.' The women and children, cows and calves all lived together in the round hut. The husband lived in solitary state in the other one. 'All the houses have a stick jutting from the roof, which is either surmounted by a cross or has a cross carved on it; practically all in this district are Christians, Catholics.'

Normally the mission to be visited was some distance away and transport had to be arranged. This was never easy. Sometimes she was driven in one of the mission cars, which were very few in number. Sometimes she got a lift in a lorry for a small fee, a common way of travelling. Sometimes she had to hire a car from Moshi which always proved complicated. The car could arrive at any time or not at all. It could come at four in the morning and waken all the nuns by loud blowing of the horn. It could come at four in the afternoon when the whole day was gone. And when it did arrive, it mightn't even be a car at all. She told Emma Bodkin about her journey to the mission at Rombo, which was typical of many.

> I had to get a car to visit a mission to contact last Thursday. You take what comes – the car ordered for 7 a.m. arrived at 2 p.m.! It was a 2 ton Chevrolet lorry, room for two with the driver – actually we travelled four in front ....
>
> I am at the moment spending a lot of time at a German convent, Kilema Mission. If I go anywhere I naturally ask if anyone wants a lift or messages – everyone does as cars are so infrequent between missions. So when I asked, I was told Reverend Mother wants to send a cow! A sister and a brother came in front with me.
>
> Well, Emma, it was a pantomime. The car came down to the convent, in front of which is a huge flower and vegetable garden. The nuns were out and about 20 natives, when the cow appeared with another native who had it on a rope. It got up to the car and then the fun began. She ran round the car and made for the crowd – we cleared. Then she broke off the rope and made up the garden path with 5 natives about in chase. She was eventually led back and when near the car escaped again and off with the crowd in pursuit. One of the sisters assisted in the capture this time.
>
> Then they put a foot-wide plank against the lorry – naturally this drew a blank. The final steps consisted in roping her legs, getting her on the ground on a board and lifting her bodily on to the lorry, not without many protests on her part! They freed her in the lorry and she nearly kicked the back out! Anyway, we did get to the mission 2 hours later safe with the cow.

Edel's account suggests that she thoroughly enjoyed the comedy. Sister Angelita, who was present as a young nun, felt that the reality must have been far from enjoyable. First of all there was the long wait of seven hours for the car. That was followed by the imposition of the cow. Most of the younger sisters felt that the Reverend

Mother showed little consideration in making the request and further delaying an already late start. Then there was the addition of an extra passenger, squeezing a fourth person into a space that could barely hold three, for an uncomfortable two-hour journey over primitive tracks.

To cap it all, Sister Angelita was told by the sister accompanying Edel that, when they finally arrived at Rombo seven hours late, the priest gave Edel a very frosty reception and showed no interest in the Legion of Mary. Even this setback was described in rosy terms by Edel. She reported to Brother Nagle, 'He is not too optimistic about the prospects. I do not think he quite realises what the Legion can do for him. However, he is in earnest and I would say sincere about doing what he can to get going.' In the event, Edel's tact as usual won the day and a Praesidium was started in Rombo.

If the mission she was visiting was a long way off or if she had a few days' work to do there, she would stay in a convent attached to the mission or in a hotel in Moshi or Arusha. Otherwise she returned to her base in Kilema and tried to be back in time for the evening meal at 7 p.m. Occasionally she looked so tired and drawn when she got back that the nuns insisted on putting her to bed straight away and brought her dinner up to her. The diary she was keeping at the time shows that they had grounds for concern. One entry begins: 'very dopy – touch of fever – sick – temp. 99.6 – took things easy – off grub.' Needless to say, there is no hint of this in any of her letters.

On one occasion, which was to become famous, she did not get back to Kilema until 11 p.m. The convent door was locked, the lights were out, the nuns were all asleep. She could not get in without waking the whole community. She decided to spend the night on the verandah, lying on a wooden bench with her coat wrapped around her.

When the nuns came down the following morning, they were astonished to find her waiting at the door. None of them would have dreamed of spending the night on the verandah: not only was it cold at that altitude, there was also a real danger from wild animals that prowled at night. They were greatly impressed by her considerate and selfless action and the story spread from convent to convent throughout East Africa.

There was, however, at least one dissenting voice. Sister Moses, the infirmarian, met her on the stairs and asked her where she had been. Edel told her she had stayed on the verandah to avoid waking the nuns. Sister Moses was not impressed and she asked Edel if she thought the sisters so lacking in charity that they would not be willing to come down and let her in. 'You work hard all day,' Edel answered, 'and I couldn't disturb your night's rest.' The sister asked her not to do it again but Edel would not promise; she said she would never be willing to disturb the sisters' sleep. She then went to the church as usual for Mass and received Holy Communion before breaking her fast

Not long afterwards, the same thing happened again. Edel was late and once more she spent the night on the verandah. Sister Moses was waiting for her when she came in and gave her a severe scolding. Then she ordered her to drink a hot cup of coffee. Edel obediently drank the coffee, though it meant she broke her fast and could not receive Communion. Sister Angelita, standing nearby, saw that her eyes were full of tears.

There may have been a slight touch of malice on the sister's part. All the same, one can understand her feelings. It does not seem to have occurred to Edel that some of the sisters might rather be woken up than have her spend the night in the open. It was even possible to see in her action an implied criticism of the sisters, as if to say that she found the cold and the beasts easier to face than the wrath of the nuns. What she did was well-meant but it may have been a little ill-judged.

Apart from this, her stay in Kilema convent was a happy one. After the evening meal each day two of the younger nuns were given permission by the Reverend Mother to spend their recreation time with her. They enjoyed her company, her good humour and her sense of fun, and they were glad of the chance to practise their English and learn some of the latest slang expressions. And they helped to cushion her shock at realising that she would be thirty years of age on 14 September 1937, as she told her family.

Last night by accident, I was talking to two of the sisters, they were talking about ages etc. and one said, 'Now you know what age I am.' I said, 'I'll be 30 tomorrow.' Then they wished me a happy feast and when I went to lunch they had a vase of violets and a holy picture at my place and a chocolate cake with white edging and my initials E.Q. on it. Wasn't it decent of them!!

The day had other surprises in store. 'I got a present of 2 pairs of Kayser stockings,' she told Leslie, 'and another present of a lovely blue photo album with mounts, so my snaps will get attention. Then a special friend of mine out here came over for the afternoon and stayed all following day, happening to be on holidays not too far away, from Nairobi.' Her diary records that Fathers Finnegan and Reidy came to Kilema that day and that she had discussions with Father Reidy the next day regarding an abridged handbook, so it is safe to assume that he was the special friend referred to.

By the end of October she had covered all the missions in the eastern part of the Vicariate and she decided to move to Arusha, from which it was easier to visit the western part. She said goodbye to the Bishop and the nuns in Kilema, especially the sisters who had shared their recreation time with her, Sisters Angelita, Gratiana, Willibald, Lutwina and Ignatius. 'Sister Gratiana and I thought she was a saint,' Sister Angelita said later, 'and we were convinced that she lived a truly holy life, to judge from her actions and her words.'

She settled into new accommodation in Arusha on 27 October. 'I came along here by lorry on Wednesday and have parked at a very nice place, private hotel, very good grub and very comfy.' She was working harder than ever, trying to visit the remaining missions before the rains came. She also had to fit in a flying visit to Nairobi for a meeting of the Curia. A letter to her family gives an idea of the hectic pace at which she was living.

Tuesday noon I hit the trail per motor lorry for Nairobi, 200 miles, I am being met about 40 miles outside it; a few visits to outside missions; the Curia on Sunday 14th, a Praesidium meeting, and back 200 miles to Arusha, next 50 miles to Moshi, next 30 miles to three missions, where I have three meetings, one at 6.30, one at 11 o'clock, and the 3rd at 4 p.m. I spend part of the day in a car. Next day back to Arusha, 50 miles; meeting on Monday and Tuesday, motor 200 miles to Nairobi and next day or the day after 200 miles to Kisumu, where I have to meet a new Bishop and start in another Vicariate, which is the same as a Diocese at home. So do not blame me if the letters are short and perhaps only postcards!

The so-called 'short rains' that year began in mid-November. They were earlier and heavier than usual and many roads were impassable. Edel decided to leave the Kiliminjaro Vicariate, abandoning plans to visit the last mission on her list, which was now unreachable. Despite this, she was well satisfied with the response she had received, though she admitted to a friend that she found the American priests a little difficult to understand. 'They are utterly different from Irish or English Fathers and as you say "temperamental", at least some of them are. I think it must be the speed at which everything appears to go in America. But they are lively and I had some good fun with them!'

By now even the main road from Arusha to Nairobi was treacherous and few cars were prepared to travel. Eventually she managed to find a seat on a rather decrepit lorry and set off about 2 p.m. on 23 November. 'The lorry I travelled in from Arusha had a leaking radiator,' she told the family, 'and every 10 miles there was a stop to put in water, a terrible job.'

As they approached Nairobi things got worse. 'The roads are in a desperate state,' she wrote to Mr Duff. 'It was quite an adventurous run coming up from Arusha to Nairobi for the last 50 odd miles.' She wisely gave no details either to him or to her family about what made the last part of the journey so adventurous. Thirty years later Father John Reidy filled in the gap in her account.

She was coming from Arusha and Father Tom Maher let me know that she was coming in a lorry. We left Nairobi in the evening, intending to meet her and take her from the lorry. We were on the road out of Kajiado in an old Dodge motor car and the mud was terrible. We thought she must have got stuck somewhere and we kept on going to meet her. It was about midnight when we met the lorry. We took her out of the lorry and transferred her to the car. She had been in the lorry since early morning and it was now around midnight. All she was worried about was us and the trouble she was causing us.

The rain was pouring down, we were covered in mud up to our eyebrows, we were stuck fast and we had to spend the night in the car. We were soaked to the skin and she was the same. She was cold and hungry and yet she kept cheerful and in good humour. There were lions all around. We killed a gazelle as a decoy and put it in the beam of the headlights. Morning came and the animal hadn't been touched, no lions had come near. Some cars came past and with their help we got free and got back to Nairobi.

We were exhausted and starving when we got there, but she was only worried about us, that no-one would suffer any ill-effects from the safari, and she wanted it kept secret so that no-one in Nairobi would know about the incident for fear that news of the safari would get back to Ireland. News about an apparent imprudence would have got the people who sent her out into trouble.

We got to Nairobi about midday. She and Father Tom Maher got out at Peter Claver's and I went to the garage to get the car washed. It really was an ordeal and we felt the effects of it though we were strong and hardy; she didn't show any. It was a lorry not a bus, but no-one got a cold as a result of the incident.

It is easy to imagine how Mrs Quinn would have reacted if she had heard how her daughter spent a night in a canvas-roofed car, cold and hungry and soaked to the skin, stuck fast in the deep African mud with hungry lions roaming all around and a sacrificial gazelle spread out in the beam of the headlights. It was certainly a time for telling less than the whole truth.

FIFTEEN

The Rolls Royce

Edel had intended to spend no more than a day or two in Nairobi before setting off on her next campaign in the Vicariate of Kisumu in western Kenya. But a combination of events delayed her departure. One was the continuing bad weather, another (though she does not mention this) must have been the need for a short breathing space. There were also matters of Legion concern to be attended to in the Nairobi area.

One of the saddest of these was the collapse of the Junior Praesidium in the Loreto School, where she was staying. It had been dogged from the beginning by the problem of getting girls of different classes and races to work together. The same problem brought it to an untimely end. In a letter marked 'Private' she told Brother Nagle how the difficulty of finding a suitable President had proved insurmountable. 'We had not a big choice and Reverend Mother was not satisfied generally with the social standing, I suppose that is how you would call it, of most of those available. That to my mind was the main factor which caused the Praesidium to close down. This reason put on paper sounds very snobbish, but I suppose one has to make allowances for the terrible class distinction that exists out here.' Though she does not say so directly, there is little doubt that she felt the Reverend Mother was herself unduly affected by the attitudes of pupils and parents.

On Friday 3 December 1937 she left for Kisumu. The roads were still bad but fortunately Kisumu was on the main railway line from Nairobi. She saved three hours by catching the train at Limuru and had a comfortable and uneventful journey. The bishop had arranged for her to stay at Kikuye in the convent of the Mill Hill sisters, who were all English with the exception of one Irish sister. As they did not know what day she was coming, there was no-one to meet her when she arrived in Kisumu at 5.30 a.m. She took a taxi from the station to the convent which was a short distance outside the town. The sisters never forgot their first impressions of her. 'I can still see Edel as she jumped out of the car and walked over to us with her swinging stride and introduced herself. "My name is Edel Quinn and I think you are expecting me. Am I in time for Mass or can I get Holy Communion?" '

She found the town of Kisumu quite charming, 'much prettier than Arusha or Moshi'. It was situated on the shore of Lake Victoria, Africa's largest lake, a vast inland sea almost the size of Ireland. From the convent she could see boats criss-crossing its calm waters and sea-planes landing and taking off. She was told that it was possible to visit most of the missions by boat even when the rains made the roads unusable.

The next morning, Saturday, she visited the Vicar, Bishop Nicholas Stam. 'The bishop here is a Dutchman, an old missionary, very nice.' The Vicariate was in the care of the Mill Hill Fathers, most of them either Dutch or English. She discussed plans with the bishop, who promised his support to her and to the Legion and specified a limited number of missions which she could visit. Before she left the house, a photograph was taken of her with the bishop and three of his priests. The bishop, sitting in the centre with purple soutane and flowing white beard, fits the picture of the old missionary to perfection.

There was a meeting of Goan Catholics on Sunday which was addressed by both Edel and the bishop. Then she set off again on the familiar routine, visiting Kakamega, Rangala, Yala, Eldoret and Kitale. Her entrance to Eldoret was made in style. 'Went up here, breathe it not, in a fishcart, but it was a de luxe model one, it was one of those small delivery vans, brand new, had only done over 3,000 odd miles. They take one or two European passengers in front with the driver and a few natives go in the back with the fish.' Her reception in general was friendly but cautious. 'One cannot rush the Dutch.' In any event, her aim was only to sow the seed before the Christmas celebrations interrupted her work. She would return in the new year, revisit the different missions and hopefully reap the harvest. She left Kisumu by native bus at 9 a.m. on the morning of Christmas Eve and reached Nairobi at 7.30 that evening in plenty of time for Midnight Mass.

The week after Christmas was an enforced holiday. All the priests felt in need of a rest and they were not interested in discussing business. She received plenty of invitations from her friends, clerical and lay. She had lunch in Peter Claver's, tennis with the Byrnes, dinner with the O'Sheas. She was brought on a picnic, taken to the cinema and 'on Thursday last went to a very good Revue that was on, all togged up in Les's evening frock complete with brocaded coat!' Some nights she slept at the Loreto Convent, others with the Precious Blood sisters in Eastleigh. It was all a little too much for her. One of her diary entries that week ends with the very Dublin expression 'jaded tired'.

She had received a letter from Frank Duff on Christmas Day. On 4 January she wrote him a long and unusually personal reply, reviewing the first full year of her mission with some satisfaction and giving all the credit to him.

I think all the results of the work out here are yours by every right, as after all I doubt if any Concilium officer but you would have suggested sending me out – and, the suggestion made, have persevered in it in the face of all the opposition, even from friends. So there is no possible doubt as to who was responsible or shouldered the burden. I am glad that the first year has justified your decision. As you say, the fact that my health has kept the same is a big proof of the effects of prayer. Because, you know, between the journeys and the big changes in altitude and climate – from very hot to very cold, and this in the same few days often – the fact that all goes well says a lot, D.G. It is not that one minds the changes or the travel a scrap, but normally the climatic quick changes are inclined to knock people about a little. However, it is a great life and I truly and thoroughly enjoy the work, and as you can guess am quite ready to carry on out here for as long as you people consider necessary or otherwise.

Her plans for the first part of 1938 were clear. She would return to Kisumu Vicariate and follow up the contacts she had made before Christmas. In February she would move on to the Vicariate of Nyeri, which was under the care of the Consolata Fathers from Italy. She had met the Vicar, Bishop Carlo Re, in Nairobi and he had promised to recommend the Legion to all his priests. She would continue there until the arrival of the rains in March made travel by road difficult. Then she would go back again and finish off Kisumu, where the lake made it easy to move around even during the rainy season.

The first part of the plan worked well. She had another meeting with Bishop Stam on 1 February and found him surprised and delighted with the progress of the Legion, especially among the Africans.

He told me I could work anywhere I liked as regards the rest of the Vicariate when I rubbed it in I only worked where he gave me permission. As I thought, he said he just confined it to these places because he did not think there really would be much scope or rather reaction to it on the native part; I do not think he meant to confine it for any other reason. I told him of course that the priests had all been most helpful, which was true, and he said, 'They should be: after all, it is to help them in their mission too.' I am to see him before I leave. Here one has to be careful about the proprieties etc. It is expected, I gather; however, it is not a burden. I return to this Vicariate when the rains start in Nyeri.

She had an unpleasant surprise when a letter arrived from Bishop Re telling him that her trip to Nyeri was off. The reason he gave was that he feared trouble among the Kikuyu tribe who might use the Legion for political purposes. Edel had already met this problem in Mangu and overcome it; however, the bishop's word was final. Having told Bishop Stam that she would be away from Kisumu for six weeks and arranged her schedule accordingly, she now found herself with an awkward hiatus to be filled.

She returned to Nairobi, where she met Bishop Heffernan, who suggested that she should finish off his vicariate by going to the island of Zanzibar. 'I got no option to refuse, it was more a command, he is very pleased I was able to fit it in.' A certain reluctance on her part could perhaps be explained by the fact that one of the priests in Zanzibar was Father O'Flynn, who had shown himself so unenthusiastic when she tried to start the first Praesidium in Nairobi.

She went to Bura to see to the formation of a Curia for the area, and then on to the port of Mombasa. The boat, a small cargo boat called the *Dumra* with room for a dozen or so passengers, left Mombasa at 5.30 p.m. and did not get to Zanzibar until 5.30 p.m. the following day. However, the calm sea and sunny weather made the voyage a pleasant one and she was relaxed and rested when she reached the island.

The whole island is bordered with cocoanut palm trees, numberless small boats and dhows are everywhere along the shore and look very picturesque with their small sails. The minute you land, you get the smell of cloves, which is the main industry. There are large groves of them all over the island.

The island is full of Arabs, and all the houses have beautifully ornamented doorways, many antique shops are about, and the houses are all full of balconies. Everywhere you go you get the smell of incense, of which a lot is burned. There are only about 150 whites all told on the island. The streets are all fearfully narrow and the houses close together. In the main street two cars could not pass each other, and in some of the other streets one car can get through if no-one stands in the street!

The tiny island, only 640 square miles in area, had a population of a quarter of a million, the great majority of them Muslim Arabs. The nominal ruler was the Sultan of Zanzibar but real power was in the hands of a British official called the Resident. There was only one Catholic mission, which included the Cathedral, the priest's house, the Precious Blood convent and the school. Edel was given a room in the convent.

On the Sunday after her arrival, 27 February, she organised a meeting for non-natives (which meant Goans) in the morning and for natives (which meant Africans) in the afternoon. She spoke as usual and asked for volunteers. Father O'Flynn attended both meetings and did his best to sabotage her efforts. At the follow-up meeting for the Goans a Praesidium was set up and Father Soares, who was himself a Goan, agreed to act as spiritual director. The follow-up meeting for the Africans was less successful, thanks to Fr O'Flynn. A young priest who was on the mission staff, Father Dan O'Leary, was impressed by Edel's patience and forbearance towards Father O'Flynn.

> He came to the meeting and showed that he didn't want it (he had often said to me in private that he didn't think Zanzibar was the place for the Legion). Her embarrassment was obvious; I can still see it on her face. At that same meeting, before it even began, Father O'Flynn kept looking at his watch and suggesting that since there were so few people there the meeting should be called off. One of the Africans there asked him, 'Why the hurry? The people will come.' Miss Quinn could have smiled but she avoided showing any sign of amusement. I myself found it very hard not to laugh.

Edel's report was more restrained. 'We had two meetings for the natives, we got nine volunteers in the town who were anxious to join, but Father O'Flynn was not satisfied with their "status" among the natives. He wanted some much older Christians, so he would not let them form a branch.' Edel had to abandon hope for the moment of a native Praesidium. She did however succeed in starting a junior Praesidium for the girls in the convent school. The spiritual director was Sister Sieglinde, a sister of Edel's friend in Kilema, Sister Angelita.

In between these events, Edel found time for a little sight-seeing.

A nurse from the hospital, Miss O'Shea, drove her to see various places of interest. Edel appreciated her kindness, even though she described her in a letter as 'the world's worst driver'. On one of their drives, Miss O'Shea almost precipitated a constitutional crisis when she came face to face with the Sultan's car in a narrow street. Miss O'Shea was unwilling to back because she had never fully mastered the art of reversing. The Sultan was unwilling to back because it would strike his dignity a mortal blow. Eventually, after immense efforts which were greatly enjoyed by a large crowd, Miss O'Shea managed to reverse into an even narrower side street and the Sultan could proceed. 'She apologised to him. He is in and out of the hospital a good deal. So though the circumstances were very undignified, I got an opportunity of a close-up view.' She left Zanzibar on 7 March in considerable comfort on the *S.S. Compiegne*, a French liner bound for Marseilles. The trip to Mombasa took only ten hours and she was able to claim a missionary's discount on her ticket: 'a 20% reduction at the expense of announcing one's vocation – what?!!'

She went at once to Nairobi for some meetings and then headed on to complete her work in Kisumu, as she had promised Bishop Stam. She caught a military train in Limuru at 9.45 p.m. which left her in Nakuru at 3.45 a.m. on the morning of 17 March, St Patrick's Day. She slept for a couple of hours, went to Mass in the mission, and then at 8 a.m. boarded a goods train bound for Kisumu. She sat in the guard's van on a large straw and wood chair provided by the station-master, serenely writing letters while thunder rolled and lightning flashed all around her. Suddenly the rains broke and a torrent of water swept in the window, soaking the page on which she was writing to her family. She tore it up and started a new page. She arrived at Kisumu at 8.15 p.m., having spent St Patrick's Day in a rain-swept guard's van. 'It is drowning the shamrock all right.'

The next day she left Kisumu for the mission at Kisii, which meant two hours in a motor launch and a thirty-mile lorry drive. It was the start of a long round of visiting and re-visiting the missions

of the Kisumu Vicariate which was to continue, with occasional in-
terruptions, for four full months. She was not always successful at a
first attempt, as at one unnamed mission, where she was received by
two priests, one Austrian and one Dutch.

I was brought in and of course given the famous morning tea.
Then we started. They told me they did to me what they did to
school inspectors – fed them up, kept them talking so that they
could not talk business. However, we did, eventually, and he had
powerful reasons etc. why he would not have it or rather need it.
Eventually he told me when he got the third curate he'd have it. It
is a real case of this year, next year.

She spent Easter Sunday at Nyabondo mission which had two
special attractions, its magnificent location and its radio set.

I had a very pleasant Easter, a meeting in the morning, a peaceful
afternoon, divided between a read and a siesta, as is the custom
out here, till tea. Then a good walk after tea along the escarpment
(I think I told you the Nyabondo mission is about 5,000 feet over
the plains) with the two priests and two dogs, one an Airedale and
the other an Alsatian. Home to a sundowner, dinner, wireless
which was pretty hopeless, mostly Church services, so we did not
listen in much, then bed. The previous night, Saturday, at the
same place we had a great variety concert ex London which included George Robey. It was most amusing and wasn't over till
about 11 p.m.

On Easter Monday she hired a car and driver and left the mission
at about 9.30 a.m. for the forty-mile journey to Kisii. After twenty
miles the car spluttered and stopped. The driver tinkered with the
engine for the best part of an hour before making the discovery that
the petrol tank was empty. 'Then the fun began,' she told her family.
'Two kids, natives, pushed us first, then we got a long run down a
hill, then five native road workers were requisitioned and they and
two others and the driver pushed the car three miles.' Then the

driver set off with a petrol can to see if he could get petrol from a European who lived four miles away while Edel lay back on the seat and wrote letters. Finally she was rescued by a priest from Kisii, Father Doyle, who came out in his car to see what had happened to her. It was after five when they sat down to a high tea at Kisii convent.

It was the kind of thing Edel had become used to, and she always made light of it in her letters. But this incident seems to have been the last straw. Once again a whole day had been lost and she had not too many days left. She talked the matter over with Father Doyle, who was the local Mill Hill superior and an experienced missionary, and he told her that the only solution was for her to buy her own car. Apart from the convenience of being able to travel freely, it would be cheaper in the long run. She could easily have bought a car with the money she had spent on trains, lorries, buses, taxis and hired cars. The following day she sat down and typed a long letter to Brother Nagle asking for permission to buy a car and giving her reasons. Up to this, she had always played down her transport difficulties. Now she had to tell the full unvarnished truth.

This is how the travelling goes. In Nairobi I was never at a loss, the Fathers there were always on tap and even anticipated when I'd need it. I think there were only about four occasions when I had to hire a car. Then Tanganyika, i.e. Kilimanjaro. There was one mission there I could get to by a lorry, just taking a seat on it, all the others I had to hire a car each time. Father Neville gave me a lift to his place twice, and Father Cromer from his mission on two occasions. As regards Kilema, whilst there I had to hire a whole lorry on two occasions, and even then it was touch and go that they came. On two other occasions there, there was a car on its last legs a brother had, and on which you could go if he was free and you paid petrol etc.

Now for Kisumu, in this vicariate since I came, on one occasion I was dropped at a mission because a priest was passing it, and on one other occasion, where a car ordered did not turn up and I was badly stuck to get to a meeting arranged, a priest at the mission gave me a lift, explaining how necessary it was to have a car oneself! Sometimes where it was only a question of 15 miles or so and I have been to great trouble trying to find a car that could be hired, to say nothing of the tough price charged, and cars were at a mission, I have not even been offered the use of one, though it was known the position I was stuck in. This is just to give you an idea of how things go, and these people are not all Dutch either and neither is it that you'd expect a lift for nothing.

The letter must have been a shock to the Legion authorities, not just for its contents but for its tone as well. This was not the sunny Edel they were used to, brushing aside every difficulty with a joke and a smile. This was an Edel worn down by constant worry and frustration to something near breaking point. Her unwillingness to complain had left them completely unaware of the difficulties she faced. She had asked them to reply as soon as possibly by air mail to Kisumu, where there was a suitable car for sale. They went one better. They immediately sent a telegram and told her to buy the car. She wrote again on 9 May to announce that she was the proud possessor of a car, though not the one at Kisumu. 'Actually a better bargain, according to the priests, turned up at Kitale, a 1932 Ford coupé, 1934 engine, re-painted, engine re-bored and new pistons, five brand new tyres, price £65. I had to settle on taking it immediately else it was gone, so I did.' Evidently her years in Callow's motor works had not been spent in vain.

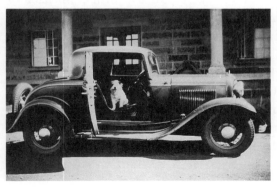

*Edel's 'Rolls Royce',
Spring 1938.*

In those days of few cars, most owners gave their cars names. Emma Bodkin's car was called Teresa. Edel christened hers the Rolls-Royce. It soon proved its worth. On 10 May she heard that Archbishop Riberi, the Apostolic Delegate, would be spending the night in Nairobi and then going on to Mombasa. She had not seen him since her original meeting with him in Dublin and there were many things she was anxious to discuss. The next morning she drove from Kitale to Nairobi, a distance of 250 miles over very variable roads, and arrived at St Austin's mission at 2 p.m., just two hours before he was due to take the train for Mombasa. She had hired an African driver, as she had not yet passed her driving test.

The meeting with the Delegate was both helpful and encouraging. When she said that the work was going slowly, he said that was the way he wanted it done, 'thoroughly and methodically'. He agreed that it was not enough to start a Praesidium; it had to be carefully nursed, even if this meant her going back for further meetings until it was functioning properly in accordance with the Handbook. 'You cannot be sure,' she told him tactfully, 'that the priest will have the time to look up the handbook on the point.'

Then they discussed the different vicariates in detail, the ones she had visited and the ones she hoped to visit. He told her about the vicars apostolic he had recently met in the Lake Victoria area and assessed the prospects. Bishop Negri of Equatorial Nile did not seem too enthusiastic. Bishop Lacoursière of Ruwenzori was a French Canadian and looked a more likely prospect. Bishop Michaud of Uganda, who had answered her letter unfavourably, was best left alone for the moment. Bishop Oomen of Mwanza was an old man and would wait to see how the Legion worked elsewhere before making a decision. Dr Riberi would be seeing the newly appointed Bishop Reesink of Upper Nile as soon as he arrived and would recommend the Legion to him. He was confident that the success of the Legion in the vicariates where it had been set up would become widely known and that this would overcome any misgivings in other vicariates.

He gave her his blessing and she drove him to the train. 'He asked re my health and was pleased I was looking so well!!' Some priests were at the station to see him off and he told them to put their energy into making the Legion work. If she had any doubts about his commitment to the Legion, they were now fully dispelled. She had a firm ally in the Pope's representative.

Shortly after this, her reluctance to complain about anyone or anything caused another surprise for Dublin. Frank Duff decided that Bishop Heffernan should be given the Legion's highest honour and declared a laureate member. When he consulted Edel, she had to tell him that the bishop had not been as helpful as might have appeared from her letters. Admittedly, he had invited the Legion to East Africa and given it his approval. But he had shown little interest in subsequent developments and had ignored invitations to Legion functions, especially when natives were involved. 'It seems to me that it would lower the value of the laureate membership, at any rate in the eyes of most of the spiritual directors of native Praesidia in Zanzibar Vicariate, if it was bestowed in this instance.' No more was heard of the proposal. Back in Kisumu, there was another two months work awaiting her as she completed her circuit of the missions. On 25 May she took her driving test.

Today I got my driving licence!! Had to go out with European Superintendent of Police, drive about a quarter of a mile, halt in case of accident, turn, give various signals and reverse a few times, was a bit weak on the latter, but he said it was a question of practice. So I am a fully fledged driver now, believe it or not. Of course I have a native driver for a few months yet – he also washes and irons my clothes so suits me fine – and polishes my boots!! Ali is his name.

Ali, who was a Muslim, did not last long. He was a good driver but had an unfortunate tendency to over-indulge in the local native beer. After one hair-raising journey, during which the car veered wildly from one side of the road to the other, Edel decided they would have to part company. A new driver, Anselmo, was at the wheel when she crossed the border from Kenya into Uganda and arrived in the town of Kampala on 22 July 1938.

SIXTEEN

Uphill in Uganda

Edel entered Uganda with a certain amount of trepidation. The country with its four million inhabitants and its network of well-established missions seemed to offer her a golden opportunity. But there were obstacles that had to be overcome. So far she had received permission to work in only one of the country's four vicariates, the Upper Nile Vicariate, and even that permission was only provisional. The previous Vicar, Bishop Campling, had resigned and Edel's permission had come from the priest temporarily in charge, Father Minderop. Whenever the new Vicar, Bishop Reesink, arrived from Europe it was possible that he might have different views.

Another cause of concern was her health. Some time in June she had what she described as a cold, which forced her to rest for about two weeks. This time she felt it was safe to tell Frank Duff and John Nagle about it, while warning them not to let anyone else know. 'The cold is now reduced,' she wrote shortly after her arrival in Uganda, 'I am in good form, D.G. The cough hasn't gone, of course, but it is always inclined to turn up. It is ever so much better since the rest-cure.' The consumptive cough had by now become a permanent part of her life.

Finally, she was worried about Mother Kevin. Mama Kevina, as she was known, was the legendary Irish nun who had founded two sisterhoods, the Franciscan Missionary Sisters for Africa and the Little Sisters of St Francis. She had worked in Uganda for thirty-five years and her influence was immense, as Edel told Frank Duff. 'Mother Kevin is known, you know, as the second Bishop of Uganda, so one treads carefully till permission comes.'

Edel must have had some reason to worry about Mother Kevin's attitude towards the Legion. She wrote to a friend in Ireland, 'She probably doesn't see how it can work amongst natives. It may be easier to explain that when speaking to her and giving examples of where it is working and the work they are doing. I believe if one can win her support it will mean a lot for the work in that part, she appears to be all-powerful.'

In the event her fears were justified. Uganda was to prove the most difficult of all her mission-fields. The endorsement from Mama Kevina that would have opened every door for her was never given. She was denied access to the other three vicariates and even in Upper Nile she met much resistance from priests and people. Her health continued to give trouble. It was a time during which her will and perseverance were tested as never before.

She stayed in the convent of Mother Kevin's sisters at Kampala on the shores of Lake Victoria. Using it as a base, she moved around the different missions in the way to which she had now become accustomed. The Rolls-Royce proved its value every day. Reports began to come back to Dublin describing priests and sisters visited and Praesidia set up. Catholic missionaries had been at work in Uganda for sixty years and the Church there was regarded as the strongest and most flourishing in East Africa. But a private letter she sent to John Nagle painted a darker picture of 'case' (i.e. lapsed) Catholics and discouraged priests.

> Since I came out, in no Vicariate have I got such a poor response in the way of numbers. The latter mean nothing, of course, and six good members are worth a lot of half-hearted ones. But if you saw the number at the general meeting at Kampala for native men, and then we got ten, and of the ten three have not turned up at the last few meetings. Of the seven left, only two are the local Baganda tribe, the others are Kenya natives, foreigners as they call them here. At Jinja it is the same, only here the number of Christians is smaller and one would not expect much.
>
> The number of 'case' people everywhere is large and of course there is consequently lots of work. But one can see from the Fathers that the number of case people makes their work difficult, and the 'good' Catholics are not keen on work as we know it.

However, if we get a few branches moving, it will be fine, but the majority of the priests are tired of forming 'associations' and look on anything new as doomed to failure, owing to the present state of their sodalities. They cannot realise how the Legion is different and only the successful working of Praesidia, where one gets permission, will convince them.

There were some lighter moments. One of these was the tea-party to celebrate the birthday of the Kabaka, the ruler of the Baganda tribe from which Uganda took its name. Edel was among those invited and she sent her sister Leslie a pen-picture of the event.

The day of the tea, I donned the mauve crepe-de-chine rig-out and my white kid shoes and set off with the lady doctor in the car. As we came in, we walked up the centre of the grounds towards the palace. Under a tree, the King was seated, behind him his sister princess, a Catholic. Each European shakes his hand and says 'Happy birthday, Your Highness' and passes on. He was dressed in a grey European suit. He is a sick man undoubtedly and they say his advisers on that account would not let him go to London for the Coronation. In previous years I believe he always stood up to greet people.

Then, when we greeted him, we moved on to a table for four for tea. Some of the priests were in just before us, so we had two at our table. When the natives greet him, they kneel on both knees. I was introduced to a Prince Joseph, Catholic, member of the royal clan. All sounds very posh, till you remember they are natives!

The slightly patronising tone of this description is found more than once in her letters to Monkstown. It must be said in explanation that it was not easy to find topics of interest for her long and regular letters to the family. Descriptions of Legion work bored them and anything remotely touching her health was better avoided. She often had to fall back on such topics as scenery, wild animals, women's fashions, and the general quaintness of the native Africans.

The result could give a lopsided picture of her own priorities. She was not in fact greatly interested in ladies' dress and fashions; but she knew that her sisters were and she catered to their interest. She knew likewise that they would not welcome informed discussion of African life and customs. What they wanted was something that would reinforce their own stereotype of the natives as primitive and childish people, who were comic when they followed their own customs and ridiculous when they followed European ones. What they wanted was funny stories and funny stories is what she gave them.

It is a pity she did not make more attempt to convey to them her own respect and love for the people of Africa. Her letters to the Legion headquarters are very different; indeed, they give the impression that if anything she preferred Africans to Europeans or Asians. Those who testified at her canonisation process could not remember her ever showing the slightest sign of racial prejudice. One can understand and forgive her for taking the easy way out when writing to her family, often late at night after a tiring and discouraging day, trying desperately to sound cheerful and full of life. Still, it is a pity.

Her letter to Leslie about the lepers in Nyenga strikes a more authentic note. There was an old English priest there, Father Mac-Loone, who gave a warm welcome to Edel and the Legion. There were about fifty lepers in the camp in varying stages of the disease. 'They are not exactly pretty to look at, though with some you'd never think there was anything wrong. Many have no fingers or toes, that is quite common, some have terrible wounds that the sisters have to dress. One man had a hole right through his hand, where bones had to be taken out as they got bad.' A Praesidium was started for the lepers and it operated quite normally. 'At the meeting we all sit down together, just as anywhere else. The president, a leper, takes the chair, the secretary, another leper, takes the notes. You don't mind a bit sitting beside them. The priests and sisters do. There are only certain kinds of leprosy that are contagious.'

The sisters caring for the lepers were from Mother Kevin's order. Mother Kevin herself remained uncommitted. Edel went to her headquarters at Nkokonjeru and addressed two meetings, one of which was attended by Mother Kevin. The two of them met on this and other occasions but Edel never tells us what views Mother Kevin expressed about the Legion. Our only reliable information comes from the testimony of Sister Mary Christina, who witnessed some of the setbacks Edel had to accept in Uganda. 'When she wanted to start the Legion at Namagunga mission, she was rebuffed by the priest. The same thing happened at Nkokonjeru. In both cases Edel Quinn accepted with resignation treatment which was not very gentle. Also Mother Kevin thought that Uganda was not ripe for the Legion, so the Servant of God got no help or cooperation even from Mother Kevin.' It must have been a great disappointment but Edel never said a word of complaint or criticism about Mama Kevina.

The new vicar, Bishop Reesink, arrived towards the end of September and Edel went to see him. She was happy to find that he was strongly in favour of the Legion and wished to see it widely established. Rather to her embarrassment, he asked her what missions had refused to have it and what reasons they had given. She told him that the priest in one mission, an Irishman, had said it was twenty years too soon for the Legion. 'Yes,' said the bishop, 'and in fifty years it would be the same and neither he nor I would be there.' She got the impression that he would mention the Legion at all the missions when he went to visit them, though he would not force them to accept it.

It is perhaps no coincidence that the situation improved after the arrival of Bishop Reesink. The combination of Edel's gentle perseverance and the bishop's support began to win the day. 'You have good fun on the rounds in this vicariate,' she told a friend. 'Many of the Fathers are Dutch and they are really very nice, though their humour is a bit broad, but by now it would take a lot to make me blush and I have learned not even to express surprise.' To convince the waverers she could point to the success of the Praesidia that had been set up. By mid-October she had good news for Frank Duff. 'The Fathers in this vicariate have practically all taken to the Le-

gion. There are only four missions left where starts have not been arranged and two of these are fairly sure to start. One won't, I know,
and the other is doubtful.' Another month or so should see her work
in Upper Nile finished.

She began to plan her next move. She would very much like to
continue in the three other Ugandan vicariates but none of them had
agreed to accept her. Bishop Michaud of Uganda (his vicariate con-
fusingly bore the name of Uganda but only covered a small part of
the country) had responded to her letter with a firm No. The other
two, Bishop Negri of Equatorial Nile and Bishop Lacoursière of
Ruwenzori, had not yet answered so she wrote to them again. By
chance she met a friendly English priest in Kampala who turned out
to be Bishop Michaud's secretary. He told her that it would do no
good to approach the bishop again and he also warned her that
Bishop Lacoursière, a French Canadian, was not likely to prove
sympathetic. 'You know,' he told her helpfully, 'French Canadians
have no love for the Irish.'

She began to consider other possibilities in the area around Lake
Victoria. She had more or less opted for the vicariate of Bukoba in
Tanganyika on the opposite side of the lake when an unexpected
proposal came from Frank Duff. Archbishop James Leen of Mauritius had been on leave in Ireland and he had asked Frank for help in
founding the Legion in his diocese. The Archbishop was now on his
way back and his ship would be calling at Mombasa on 31 December. The proposal was that Edel should join the ship, accompany the
Archbishop to Mauritius and begin her work there under the best
possible auspices. Did she think this was feasible?

Edel thought it was more than feasible. It seemed an ideal time to
go to Mauritius. The period after Christmas was always a difficult
one as priests were on holiday or on retreat. She might as well use it
for travelling. Moreover, the ship would call at various ports in Tanganyika and Madagascar and Edel could make useful contacts there
with the Archbishop to lend his support. She made inquiries about
the fare and found that with missionary discount it would cost £23

one-way. She asked Frank to wire her immediately. 'If you say Go I will understand to arrange for Mauritius, if you say Remain, I will go on to next Vicariate, i.e. Bukoba.'

Frank received the letter on 7 December. He sent a wire at once: 'Go Mauritius Writing Duff.' She received the wire the same day and immediately wrote back to say she couldn't go after all. She was in bed in Kampala with a bad attack of malaria.

The disease had struck the previous week while she was visiting missions in the Eastern Province. 'You know the Eastern Province is a hotbed for malaria. Mother Kevin told me recently she never went up there that she did not come back with a touch of fever.' The doctor in Kampala, a friendly Irishman by the name of O'Sullivan, ordered her to bed at once. Even after the fever had gone, she would still need absolute rest for two weeks. Mauritius was out of the question for the time being. Edel accepted the inevitable with her usual good grace.

> I am at the convent here, which has been my headquarters since I came to Uganda, so I am quite at home, eating and sleeping. It will amuse you to know that I am at present in a state of being always hungry, the usual reaction after fever, believe it or not, it is funny; and I am kept well supplied! They are all very good to me and the Convent chaplain – who is a Legion spiritual director and whose father is in the Legion in Middlesbrough – from the day I went to bed brought me Holy Communion. (The sisters have not the privilege every day when they are sick.) The door of my room opens on to the chapel and so it is left open during Mass so I miss nothing! So you see that even though it is only for some days, I am as well off in bed as up, as regards Mass. I am dying to be on the job again though – but have plenty to do in the way of letters etc. to Praesidia out here just at present so the 14 days will slip by quickly.

She wrote Christmas letters to all her family and friends, omitting any reference to her malaria. She was still resting but making good

progress when Christmas came round. Christmas Eve at 7.30 was
the time when the sisters exchanged gifts. 'Along came Reverend
Mother with my tray, if you please: a native bark-cloth handbag; a
duck that winds up as a joke, moving neck; a fancy book marker; a
special parcel from Mother Kevin – two pairs silk stockings, a dozen
handkerchiefs and a sachet with a card; and then I had a very dainty
decorated china jar containing pot-pourri from doctor's wife; 2 lbs
chocs from some one else; a crepe-de-chine or rather georgette
necktie; and there you are.'

Then came midnight Mass followed by a supper of cake and wine
followed by bed at 4 followed by 'brekker in bed' at 8 followed by
Pontifical High Mass at 9. After a lunch which included such traditional fare as plum pudding and brandy sauce she was glad to escape
to her room for a good lie-down.

January saw her on the road again, this time with a change of
driver. Anselmo, though not given to drink, had proved unreliable in
many other ways, damaging the car, forgetting the luggage, even
stealing oranges from the mission gardens. On 21 January her new
driver brought her to Nkokonjeru, where Archbishop Riberi was
paying a visit. She arranged to leave Kampala at 8.30 a.m., as she
hated to be late for a meeting.

At 8.30 a.m. along came a Reverend Father from another mission
who is just going home to England on leave. He said goodbye to
me, gave me a few parcels for another mission and departed, asking if I would give him a lift down town. I said, 'Yes.' He said, 'I
must shave first.' 'Well,' I said, 'I will give you ten minutes but
cannot wait longer as I have a trip of 170 miles to do before 7
p.m. including an interview.' That would be all right. Over he
went to the mission.

I gave him five minutes and went over after him. I knew my
man. I saw him wandering round with a sunhelmet in his hand,
still unshaven, so I tackled him. He had got another good idea. He
wanted to go to Kenya and, as I was going close to the border,
might he come along? I gasped, because he had to pack. I was

rather reluctant but he said it would be most convenient. Only he first had to see some Father and fix up a sermon he had promised to give the following day. Finally, one hour later, I left the convent, and when we got to Kampala he had to shop a little. I was by then long past the stage of even pretending to be polite, as I had the appointment with Mgr Riberi and you can never be sure of not getting a puncture etc.

Fortunately they had no punctures and she was in time for her meeting with the Delegate. He produced a map of Africa and together they plotted her moves for the next twelve months. Her work in Uganda would soon be finished, as the Vicars of Ruwenzori and Equatorial Nile had at last been in touch with her and told her that their people were not sufficiently developed to work the Legion system. She agreed with the Delegate that it would best to postpone Mauritius until she could get copies of the French edition of the Legion Handbook, which was due to be published shortly. French was the language of Mauritius and her work there would go much more smoothly if her literature was in French. The same argument applied to Bukoba, which was in the charge of White Fathers from France.

The Delegate's suggestion was that as soon as she had finished in Uganda, she should go to the Prefecture of Meru in Kenya, where an Italian priest had started the Legion on his own initiative. After that she could make for Tanganyika, taking a second look at the Praesidia she had founded in Kilimanjaro, then moving towards the coast and covering the Vicariates of Bagamoyo and Dar-es-Salaam. The port of Dar-es-Salaam would be a convenient place to catch a boat for Mauritius when the time was ripe. It was a daunting schedule and it suited her down to the ground.

It was not until the end of February that she had finished everything she wanted to do in the Vicariate of Upper Nile. On 1 March 1939 she paid her last visit to Bishop Reesink. When she said goodbye, he answered, 'Well, let's hope for the best!' Greatly daring, she also went to the neighbouring Vicariate of Uganda to pay a courtesy call on Bishop Michaud, who had ruled out the Legion from the very beginning. 'He seemed pleased I had called to say goodbye (that may be because I was going to leave him in peace!) ... We got no further re his own vicariate at the interview but when and if I do get back this way again, the way is always open to a call and then one could talk of how it has gone with his neighbours and ask him if he would not change his mind.'

SEVENTEEN

Shadows of War

On her way to her next destination, Meru, Edel passed through the Vicariate of Kisumu. This gave her an opportunity of visiting many of the Praesidia which she had set up the previous year and seeing how they had fared in the meantime. On the whole, she was satisfied with what she saw, though there were a number of difficulties which had to be attended to. One was the problem of finding suitable secretaries among an African population that was still largely uneducated.

> Out here in parts it is really a difficulty getting someone to write the minutes, and when you do get one who can take notes, but slowly, it takes him often two hours to write it out etc. I have been asked if in really extreme cases, he would not be allowed to do this as his Legion work. Mind, it is a real difficulty, as it is a real job for some of these people. It was so hard to get it done in one mission that yesterday the Father asked me would it not be possible to cut it out altogether and as an alternative suggested what I have asked ... Your comments will be appreciated!

She was never willing to compromise on even the smallest point of the Legion rules without first consulting Dublin. Frank Duff gave her permission to count the secretary's job as Legion work where the situation warranted it. He was often more flexible than he was given credit for.

She got to Meru on 25 March, Feast of the Annunciation, an auspicious date for a Legion beginning. Meru was a comparatively recent development with less than a dozen missions. It had not yet been made a Vicariate but was still a Prefecture, which meant it was headed by a priest who was not a bishop. It was staffed by the Consolata Fathers from Italy and the Prefect was Monsignor Giuseppe Nepote-Fus. After her disappointments in Nyeri and

Equatorial Nile, she may have been a little wary of Italian priests. However Meru proved to be a delightful and rewarding experience after the uphill slog in Uganda.

One of the Meru priests, Father Bertolino, had already set up a Legion Praesidium in his mission at Imenti. His enthusiasm had infected the Prefect, who received Edel with great cordiality and offered her every assistance. With Father Bertolino as her guide, she went on a breakneck tour of all the missions. Everywhere she went, she found that the priests and sisters were prepared for her arrival and had organised meetings for her to address. Her only difficulty was that few of the priests and hardly any of the sisters spoke English, which made communication difficult. At some missions, she just about managed to talk to the sisters in her very inadequate Swahili.

Another mission, the sisters knew neither English or Swahili. I had dinner with the Fathers etc. but about 10 o'clock went to bed. It was a mountain mission about 5,000 feet up, very foggy and damp. I told the sisters in Swahili, the only thing I could try on them, that I did not want any more to eat or drink. I went to bed, locked the doors, put out the lights – about 20 minutes afterwards a knock at the door and here were the three sisters with one tray on which was a cup of hot milk. All I was afraid was that if I managed to drink the hot milk, which I never can take, that I'd probably be sick before they left the room. However, slowly I got it down and bowed them out, and no ill effects. It is funny to have three silent smiling sisters watching you get through a cup of anything!

She left Meru shortly after Easter, having finished her work there in less than three weeks. She summed up the results in a few words for John Nagle. 'The senior Praesidium at Imenti had grown to 60 so a second Praesidium was formed from it, and Praesidia also started at Chuka, Igoji, Kabone, Kikinduri and Tigania. The prayers were translated into Meru by Father Bertolino and are being printed on the tesserae.' Never before or since did she achieve so much so effortlessly and in so short a time.

After triumph came humiliation. Archbishop Riberi was anxious that she would made a second attempt to start in Nyeri Vicariate. He spoke to Bishop Re and arranged that Edel would visit one mission where the prospects seemed good. Edel went and found herself up against a brick wall. When she met the priest in charge, he told her he had started a lay organisation of his own and felt that it was too soon for the Legion. However, Edel was allowed to address a meeting of local Catholics, at which the head teacher repeated all the priests's arguments against starting the Legion.

At the end of the meeting, she followed her usual practice and suggested that she come back after the people had had time to decide whether they wanted the Legion or not. The priest said it would take them two weeks to decide and he would write and let her know the result. She returned to Nairobi and two days later got a letter from him saying they had decided against it. 'The whole business was a farce,' she told John Nagle. 'I knew from what he said that he never wanted to give it a chance, though the Bishop did.'

She left Nairobi in the middle of May. She was not to see it again for nearly four years. She spent the next few weeks retracing her steps through Kilimanjaro Vicariate, visiting Arusha and Moshi and Kilema and Rombo and all the other places where she had been the year before. She met spiritual directors, sat in at meetings, encouraged Legion officers. She was guided by the same motto that guided Pope John XXIII: see everything, correct a little, ignore a lot. She led by example rather than by word. When others saw her zeal and dedication, they felt their own enthusiasm rekindled.

Her tact never failed. While she insisted that the Handbook must be followed, she did it so gently and humbly that she disarmed all opposition. She was profuse in her gratitude to directors and officers, even when she had little to be grateful for. A typical incident occurred at a Praesidium she was attending when one of the members said to the spiritual director, 'It would be a help if you could come to the meetings, Father.' Though the remark was made in Swahili, Edel understood it. But she thought it more tactful to keep her face blank for the sake of the priest's feelings.

From Kilimanjaro she went to the sea-coast to the port of Tanga where she had not worked before. Though Tanga was in Tanganyika, it was part of Bishop Heffernan's vicariate. She held two meetings to call for volunteers, one for natives, one for non-natives. The responses could hardly have been more different. With great difficulty, she managed to scrape together seven members for the non-native Praesidium, all of them Goans. There were still quite a few German Catholics living in Tanga since the days of the German Empire, but she noted that many of them had stopped coming to Mass since the rise of the Nazi regime. In complete contrast, forty-four joined the native Praesidium and she found herself hoping that some of them would not last too long.

From Tanga she sailed north to Mombasa. Here again she was involved mainly in maintenance work. Archbishop Riberi was in residence at the Delegation and she had another meeting with him, which she reported at great length to Frank Duff. The topic was one which they had discussed before, the relation between the Legion and what was called Catholic Action. There appeared to be a lobby in the Vatican which wished to deny that the Legion was a legitimate form of Catholic Action. It was alleged that the Jesuits were behind this, because they were unhappy at the way the Legion was gradually supplanting their own lay organisation, the Children of Mary Sodality. Both Edel and the Delegate felt that this might lie behind some of the resistance to the Legion among sections of the clergy in East Africa.

By the end of July she had finished in Mombasa and was free to do what she liked doing best: opening up new territory. On the Delegate's advice, she headed off for two coastal vicariates in Tanganyika, Bagamoyo and Dar-es-Salaam. She had not received permission to work in Bagamoyo, which was looked after by Dutch Holy Ghost Fathers, but Bishop Bernard Hilhorst had at least agreed to meet her and she was hopeful that she would be able to win him round.

She arrived at Morogoro, where the bishop lived, on Wednesday 26 July 1939 after a drive of 172 miles. She saw him and arranged to have a formal meeting with him next morning. By now she was becoming an expert on dealing with bishops and she knew that it was unwise to make too much mention of the Delegate's support. 'Bishops are bishops,' she told Frank Duff, 'and of course the Delegate is the Delegate, but still the former prefer to act on their own, or at least that one should think they do. So the less they know that one is acting on his direct instructions regarding any matter concerning their territory the better.'

They had a free and frank discussion. The bishop mentioned the various objections he had to the Legion: old mission superiors would find it difficult, the people would not take to it, too many previous organisations had been tried and failed. Even the fact that Bishop Heffernan had sponsored the Legion seemed to rankle with him ('There are wheels within wheels,' she noted). Little of this was new to her and she answered all his questions patiently and tactfully. Gradually he came round to her point of view. When she finally asked if she could go ahead, he answered somewhat grudgingly, 'You can try it, it can't do any harm if it's under Our Lady's protection.'

Once having given his permission, he proved surprisingly supportive. He kept in constant touch with her, advising her on the best missions to try, producing maps to help her plan her journeys, and asking afterwards how she had been received. Once again, her car proved invaluable. Her new driver, Aloisi, was adept at mending punctures and making minor repairs. He managed to deliver her safely at all the missions, with the exception of Tunungo, which presented special problems.

I don't think I told you how one goes to this mission of Tunungo that I was staying in last. First, the road is the last word in ruts. Then at journey's end there is a river and the mission is fifteen minutes' walk from this. Over the river one's baggage and one-self must be carried. So first we leave the car and the driver, the latter sleeps at a house beside the car. Then we get out one suit-case, which one native puts on his head. Next comes the type-writer and small dispatch case, taken by another native on his head. The rest is left in the car and then, surrounded by the local children and about twenty men and women, we proceed to the river's edge. I pick out the two tallest and heftiest men and they join hands whilst I grab each round the neck and we start. The journey is only about 100 yards but the river is not exactly level and at times one is quite sure of getting a ducking. However, I have now got across safely five times.

The last time I came down from the mission, two mission boys carried the luggage. And then I had to get over. I was in a hurry. A tall native came out from a side path and I asked if he would take me across. So I just did pick-a-back on him and had both arms round his neck and my legs round his waist for a grip and so got across with the luggage – but the position is not graceful and one feels most undignified but when no-one looks on, it is O.K. I forgot to tell you that in the first instance when one gets safely across all the audience of kids and people clap their hands and shout!

There was no place in Bagamoyo where one could buy a newspa-per on the day it was issued. For the latest news she had to rely on the radio in Morogoro mission. During that month of August 1939 everyone listened in anxiously as the situation in Europe deterio-rated. Hitler was preparing to invade Poland, though Britain and France warned they would declare war on him if he did. It seemed likely that Italy would ally itself with Germany if war did break out.

These events had their repercussions in Tanganyika, where some of the local Germans supported Hitler, others opposed him. One day Edel rescued a motorist who had been stranded on the roadside for twenty hours with a punctured tyre. It turned out that he was a Jew-ish dentist, who had been forced to flee Germany with his wife and

family. 'He had fought during the Great War and been wounded and
on top of all that was told he was not a German racially.' She got
Aloisi to mend the puncture for him and he went gratefully on his
way.

Of more immediate concern to Edel was the effect that war would
have on the missions. She told Frank Duff that most enemy aliens
would be interned, including priests and brothers. Sisters would
probably be left alone, as long as they stayed in their missions. She
herself would continue her work as normal. If it became too difficult
in East Africa, she would move on to Mauritius or Nyasaland or
Northern Rhodesia. If they were no longer able to send her money
from Ireland, she would support herself by taking a job. 'But as long
as there is Legio work anywhere – home or abroad – to be done,
whole or part-time, I count it as a privilege to be able to do it. For
me, the Legio comes before everything.'

Hitler invaded Poland on 1 September 1939. Two days later,
Britain and France declared war on Germany. Mussolini's Italy remained neutral for the time being. The British authorities in East Africa began rounding up German residents, but an agreement was
made that German priests and brothers could remain at liberty as
long as they gave an undertaking not to leave their missions. It was
also stipulated that the superior of each mission must not be a German. As far as Edel herself was concerned, the main problem was
the restriction on the sale of petrol. She succeeded in getting official
recognition as a missionary, which gave her the right to a petrol ra-
tion for her work.

She continued her travels in the Bagamoyo Vicariate and by the
end of October could report the founding of seven senior Praesidia
and one junior, with the possibility of one or two more. She felt a little disappointed with the result, but when she happened to meet the
Delegate who was passing through Morogoro, she found he was
very satisfied. 'Considering he had not even expected a permission
for the vicariate, I suppose it was something.'

At the same time, she was visiting some of the outlying missions of the Vicariate of Dar-es-Salaam, which were close to Bagamoyo. Her first encounter with the Vicar, Bishop Edgar Maranta, a Swiss Capuchin, was memorable. On the road to Dar-es-Salaam three leaves of her car's front spring snapped. Aloisi managed to bind the spring with cord, using a branch as a splint. They set off again very slowly and it was 7.30 and pitch dark when they got to the town. She went to an Irish contact, Father J. J. McCarthy, who brought her to the mission to see the bishop. She apologised for her late arrival and explained about the car. He told her he would see about it in the morning. She left it in the mission garage for the night.

Next morning at 8 a.m. the bishop appeared in the garage dressed in full overalls and started to work. Edel went in twice to see how he was getting on but all she could see was a pair of feet sticking out from underneath the car. Eventually at 6 p.m. he declared the work completed. He had got one new leaf and moulded two others to fit, as well as putting in clamps to hold the battery more firmly in place. It appeared that cars were his passion and tinkering with them his favourite form of relaxation.

Father McCarthy, a Holy Ghost priest, was Catholic Education Secretary for Tanganyika. He became one of Edel's strongest supporters. In a letter to Ireland he wrote: 'Miss Quinn is an extraordinary individual, courageous, zealous and optimistic. She wanders round in a dilapidated Ford, having for sole companion an African driver. When she returns home, she will be qualified to speak about the missions and the missionaries, having really more experience than any single missionary I know. She is a credit to the country she comes from. You may tell that to any Legionary friends whom you may happen to know in Dublin.'

Legion friends in Dublin soon let Edel know about his remarks. Her reaction was characteristic. She ignored the embarrassing compliments and pretended to take offence at his reference to her 'dilapidated car'.

There are a few patches on the wings put on with nails, but that is not unusual out here. The inside paint work is a unique shade of purple, got by mixing left-over scraps of paint, I was told, and comes in now and then for comment. The original set of tyres were new when the car was bought but have worn out since, two new tyres had been bought last May, but two of the original ones were still on in September last, when they let me in for a series of seven punctures in one day on a safari, after which it was obvious their day was done. I got as a stop-gap second-hand ones, it was the time when all motor parts were strictly controlled, however in the new year I will probably have to get two new ones. I believe under permit one could buy them. However, no hurry. The engine is good. Every garage the car was in testified to that fact unsolicited, and others also. The car has weathered hills and roads you could have no conception of, has been stuck in mud, always a possibility out here when the rains are on, it has had petrol troubles and parts requiring renewal of course – but 'dilapidated'? No, sir! It also has the advantage, being a coupé, that if one ever was stuck in the blue with it, one could spend the night inside it in safety, because unlike other cars it would be lion proof.

While in Dar-es-Salaam she stayed with the Swiss sisters at the mission. She appreciated their kindness but she was beginning to miss the Irish faces and voices of Kenya. She liked to visit Father McCarthy, who was not only Irish himself but had an African servant who could make strong hot tea and ham sandwiches in the best Irish style. 'I often drop in and gossip, as we have both travelled the same parts and met the same people and it is fun comparing notes. One cannot gossip with other nationalities but with an English or Irish person one can.'

She remained in Dar-es-Salaam for Christmas. On Christmas Day she and Father McCarthy were invited to a traditional Christmas dinner with an Irish couple and their two children. In the evening she returned to the convent where there were games in the children's room, songs, forfeits and musical chairs. She was given presents of a georgette head-scarf and a carved native box containing a dozen handkerchiefs.

The parcel that gave her most pleasure was one that arrived shortly before Christmas and contained nine copies of the Legion Handbook in French. The French edition was now in print and further copies were being sent to Mauritius to await her arrival there. There was no reason to delay any longer her visit to Mauritius. She had started ten Praesidia in the Vicariate of Dar-es-Salaam, six senior native, two junior native, one senior non-native and one junior non-native. She felt she had done as much as she could there for the moment.

She began to inquire about the possibility of getting a boat and found that one was expected between 6 and 9 January. The precise date was not announced in advance for reasons of wartime security. She bought a ticket and packed what she needed for the journey, leaving some of her clothes and books behind. The car also had to be left behind. 'The mechanical-minded bishop is taking it at the mission, and will have battery out, car covered, tyres looked after at intervals etc. I am just to drop a line when I am coming back and he will have the battery charged!'

Aloisi, the driver, was sent home. She did not intend to employ him again. He had spent most of Christmas in an alcoholic haze, the third time this had happened. Moreover, she found he had been borrowing money from the mission, saying he was hungry and only got 25 shillings a month, whereas he was actually getting the going rate of 40 shillings. He went back to Uganda on the Friday train.

EIGHTEEN

Island of Flowers

Edel left Dar-es-Salaam on 9 January 1940 and arrived in Port Louis, capital of Mauritius, on the 22nd. The tiny island, the size of an Irish county, was set in the middle of the Indian Ocean, five hundred miles to the east of Madagascar and more than a thousand miles from the African mainland. Discovered by the French and then captured by the British, it had a bewildering mixture of races and religions among its 400,000 inhabitants. France was still the strongest influence. The language generally spoken was French and most of the people were at least nominally Catholic.

The voyage was uneventful and gave her a much-needed opportunity for a rest. She ate, read and slept for most of the time. There were occasional annoyances. One was a crying child who shared her cabin for part of the voyage. Another was an amorous gentleman who pestered her with his attentions. Her great joy was that there was a priest among the passengers and she was able to attend Mass every morning.

There was a reception committee to meet her when she left the boat in Port Louis. In addition to three Irish priests, there were the President General of the Society of St Vincent de Paul and the President of the Catholic Union. Having seen her safely through customs, the latter drove her to meet the Bishop of Port Louis, Archbishop James Leen of the Irish Holy Ghost Fathers.

Edel already had a link with the Archbishop. No doubt she told him that she knew his brother, Father Edward Leen, who had been Dean and then President of Blackrock College while her brother Ralph was a student there. Discretion would have prevented her from adding that she had decided against him as her spiritual director, when Mary Martin recommended him. She found the archbishop considerably less formidable than his brilliantly intellectual brother and quickly struck up a good working relationship with him.

He was the first bishop since Bishop Heffernan to invite her to his diocese without any prompting on her part and, unlike Bishop Heffernan, he was to give her unfailing support all during her stay.

Her driver then brought her to the Pension Dupont in Vacoas and in a typically Mauritian gesture presented her with a bunch of carnations before leaving. The Pension Dupont was a private hotel in the hills above Port Louis, chosen by the archbishop because it was cooler and healthier than the coast. It was situated beside the Loreto Convent where Edel would have preferred to stay. She felt the Pension was a little expensive and she missed the religious atmosphere of a convent and the presence of the Blessed Sacrament. To make matters worse, she found that the man who had pestered her on the boat was among the hotel guests and still not prepared to take no for an answer.

Her first task was to publicise the arrival of the Legion. The archbishop arranged to have a special issue of the diocesan magazine *La Vie Catholique* devoted entirely to the Legion of Mary. It was up to her to provide the copy. She spent four full days sitting in front of the Baby Empire, racking her brains for material. She described the history of the Legion and the different kinds of work it engaged in, she paraphrased sections of the Handbook about the organisation of the Legion, the different degrees of membership, the conduct of meetings, the prayers and the spirituality, and she gave an account of the three years she had already spent as a Legion envoy in Africa. It was all taken away and translated into French and published with a specially designed cover. She was happy with the result, especially since she still had only nine French handbooks to distribute.

She began the usual round of visiting parishes, talking to priests, addressing meetings and calling for volunteers. She tried to remember the French lessons she had taken under Pierre Landrin's direction and day by day she became more fluent in speaking and more quick to understand, though never really at ease. She got to know more about the country and the people and she found that they were locked into a class system every bit as rigid as the one that had caused her so much trouble in Nairobi.

The colour question is acute and is more difficult in some towns than others. One might say it cramps every project that is tried. The white Mauritians number I believe about 5,000 and are the descendants of the French settlers for the most part. Then one gets the mixture after that. You have the Indian and Chinese population. All the shops practically are Chinese-owned, many of the latter are Catholics. The Indians are for the most part workers in the sugar plantations and are scattered all over the island; there are three priests looking after them only. Then there is the Creole population, whose ancestors were the slaves brought from Madagascar and Africa and who have the faith only for over 100 years; in the early days I heard that these slaves were not even allowed into the churches for Mass on Sunday.

Questions of colour and class cropped up constantly in the formation of Praesidia. Some of the whites simply refused to join a branch with members of other races. The archbishop agreed that the Curia, when it was set up, would include all races. This was an advance on Nairobi, where two Curias had to be formed. But the underlying attitudes still remained unchanged. 'Really the pettiness of the white attitude to the coloured, and the attitude of the latter to the other variations among themselves, is terrible. Yet it is surprising the people who stand up for it after experience. The plea is that if this attitude had not been maintained there would not be any white people now.'

One of her first allies was a newly ordained priest, the curate in her local parish of Vacoas. Father Jean Margéot, twenty-four years of age, was a white Mauritian, just returned from Rome with a theology degree, personable, talented and full of zeal. He was impressed by her prayerfulness each morning in the parish church, where she attended Mass before beginning her day's work. When she asked about the possibility of founding a Praesidium in the parish, he gave her every assistance and they soon had three Praesidia in operation. There were occasions when his zeal outran his discretion, but he found her always understanding and patient.

I gave a sermon on the Legion in the hope of getting new members for an already existing men's Praesidium. I heard afterwards that the congregation got the impression that it was some new mutual benefit society. The result was that some forty men answered the appeal and managed to squeeze themselves into the presbytery parlour. The whole thing was clearly a mistake. Miss Quinn was very tactful and discreet. She said that this time they would not read the minutes of the previous meeting and gave no sign of impatience. She remained completely self-controlled. The meeting carried on somehow or another and the men who came that day were never seen again. The incident was closed.

There were difficulties. Some of them were old difficulties, such as the reluctance of the French priests to accept an organisation that had not come from France. There were travel difficulties too. The island was small and the roads were good but public transport was unreliable. Buses had a habit of waiting until all the seats were filled and this made for endless delays. Most of the time she used taxis, which were expensive.

Other difficulties were quite new. The archbishop was keen to have some kind of uniform that the Legionaries could wear on public occasions to show they were members of the Legion. Edel remembered the cloak that the Legionaries had worn in Lourdes and asked John Nagle if something similar could be adapted for use in Mauritius. He wrote back to say that the cloak was used only in Lourdes and could not be used anywhere else. 'I hope that the Archbishop will not be disappointed at our decision. As I explained to you in my letter, the Concilium had already ruled on the matter and, as you will realise, I have no power to alter a ruling given by the Concilium.' Edel did not question the decision, whatever her personal views. For her the word of the Concilium was final.

A graver difficulty concerned the ban on giving money or other material help as part of Legion work. This was a point on which

Frank Duff was unyielding. 'Material relief must not be given,' he wrote in the Handbook. 'The visits of an organisation which gives relief will seldom be welcomed by those who do not need relief. They will fear lest such a visitation would label them in the eyes of their neighbours as benefiting in some material way. So the Praesidium which earns the name of relief-giving will quickly find its field of work narrowed exceedingly. Material relief may be to other societies a key which opens. It is the key with which the Legion shuts itself out.'

Edel did not question this principle. Her Mauritian Legionaries did. It was a society in which hand-outs seemed to be an integral part of life. The new Legionaries found it hard to envisage a religious organisation which did not give alms. As a result, 'instead of trying to get a mentality against giving, they try and find a means to circumvent the rule.' She gave John Nagle some examples.

On this relief question I do not know if I have overstepped the bounds in strictness. A big work here is Catechism teaching in the homes of Legionaries, because some children or adults cannot attend fixed classes. (Many were doing this work all over the island on their own, it is a crying need.) The minute some people took up this work for the Legion, they started giving the children who came to them tea and bread every morning, or fruit etc. I said that was against the rules. It was equivalent to paying them to come. I said that from the Handbook, where it spoke of the merit card system, they could occasionally give them a reward for good attendance and be quite in order; but daily, no.

You see, even the priests here say it is dreadful, that they get a sick call, give extreme unction and viaticum, and, immediately after receiving, the sick person will ask for money. So bad was it that one priest told me he made it a rule never to give anything. Sometimes it was difficult to know if they were really in good faith demanding the sacraments. It sounds extreme and difficult to credit but it is true.

Everywhere you go, if you speak to these people they ask for money. In the hotel where I am staying, various members of the staff have tried to borrow money at different times. If you speak even ordinarily politely to them, in the next breath you get 'Give me sous, clothes, shoes.' Believe this or not, but the hotel house-keeper, a respectable coloured woman, came to my room the other day. I happened to be there. She put some tiny violets in a small vase I have before a statue of Our Lady. Then she said, 'Mademoiselle, give me a rupee.'

Even the new Curia for Mauritius, which was set up in April, disagreed with her on this. The president said he would write to the Concilium and explain that the condition of the poor in Mauritius was different from anywhere else. The only one who backed her up was the priest who had been appointed spiritual director to the Curia, her friend Father Margéot. 'He is very helpful, speaks English perfectly, being a Mauritian knows his people perfectly, which is also something! He realises this difficulty too and will fight it. Really there were times when I was nearly at a loss how to reply to the various methods of evasion they proposed, and not the people only, but some of the spiritual directors.'

The first Acies was held in the cathedral at Port Louis on Sunday 19 May. The Archbishop was present, with twenty spiritual directors, two hundred and ninety three active Legionaries and sixty auxiliary members. The Loreto Mother Provincial was there, with sisters from the different Loreto convents where junior Praesidia had been set up. Edel reported that the Archbishop was pleased and surprised at the number who took part. He had only one reservation. 'You know, there's one thing missing,' he said. 'What's that, Your Grace?' 'The purple cloaks.'

She felt that her work in Mauritius was coming to its end and she started to plan her next move. Because of the war, boats were few and passenger space limited. There were two French colonial islands which looked promising if she could get to them. One was the little island of Réunion, similar to Mauritius in size and population and about two hundred miles away. The other was the huge island of

Madagascar. Edel's ship had put in at several ports there on the voyage to Mauritius and she had made some useful contacts.

There was also the difficulty of getting the Archbishop's consent to her departure. She had originally intended to spend three or four months there. Now he was asking her to stay until Christmas. 'Promise me you won't leave till everything is all right,' he said. It was an awkward dilemma. Staying on would just mean starting more junior Praesidia, setting up youth clubs, helping existing Praesidia to expand in new work directions. 'To my mind the various priests, presidents and Curia can do this,' she wrote. 'After all, I suppose an envoy's work is just opening the way.' At the same time, she did not want to disappoint the Archbishop to whom she owed so much. 'Monsignor Leen is without exception the finest bishop I have met, and the most helpful from the Legion point of view.' Eventually they reached a compromise and Edel agreed to stay until after the Feast of the Assumption of Our Lady, 15 August.

The weather grew cooler in June, winter in the southern hemisphere. 'I have had vests knitted which I wear, plus one knitted silk and wool cardigan, plus one cardigan in heavy blanket wool home-knitted, plus a coat, so I should be warm!' She succeeded at last in leaving the Pension Dupont, which in addition to its other drawbacks was cold and damp. Her new home was a small house in the grounds of the Convent of Marie Reparatrice, that happened to be temporarily vacant. She managed to fit in a three-day retreat which was organised by the convent and preached by a Jesuit. She calculated that it was her first retreat in four years.

The Feast of the Assumption was to be marked by an important event, the dedication of a new shrine in honour of Mary Queen of Peace. A site had been chosen on a hillside overlooking the sea and a large statue of the Blessed Virgin holding the world in her hands had been brought from Italy. There would be a great procession to the shrine in which all the Catholic organisations would take part, including the newest one, the Legion of Mary. The Archbishop's request for cloaks for the Legion had been made primarily with this procession in mind. 'The Legionaries have the Standard to follow, if not the cloaks,' Edel wrote on 4 August. 'It will be a great event on the island, the statue has already been erected, and given a day without a breeze all should go well.' In the event, all did not go well, as Edel informed John Nagle.

I may as well tell you that the Legion section of the procession nearly wrecked the order of the said procession. I do not think I have ever been more ashamed of anything, though it could have been worse. The Curia President had the Standard of course, and the Legionaries, active and auxiliaries, were all together. A conservative estimate of their number would be about 350. The Children of Mary, a fair number, who here wear no cloaks but white dresses and veils, were in front, another section came in between, we came next in ordinary dress, and after us came the Mères Chrétiennes, all in black.

We had walked a fair distance and came to a turn where we had to walk right to the top, to the shrine, through a narrow street. Immediately the onlookers began to join in with the Legionaries, in spite of all the few stewards could do. Instead of an orderly group three wide, each line stretched across the street haphazard. It was bad. You see, only definite organisations had the right of walking first right up to the shrine. The general public were to fall in after the archbishop, the priests, the Vincent de Paul etc., but without badges Legionary and non-Legionary looked the same.

She didn't say, 'If you had let them wear cloaks, this wouldn't have happened.' She didn't say, 'I told you so.' But John Nagle can hardly have failed to get the message.

By now it was clear that there was no possibility of getting a boat to either Réunion or Madagascar. There was a boat going to Durban in South Africa early in September and she decided to book a passage on it. South Africa was not part of her territory but from there she could make for Nyasaland, which was. After that she could work her way through Northern Rhodesia and the southern and western vicariates of Tanganyika.

A farewell Mass was said for her in the Cathedral on 28 August, attended by many Legionaries. Afterwards there was a reception in a nearby hall at which she was showered with presents and, to her great embarrassment, made the subject of several speeches of thanks. She even had to make a short speech herself. Still, it was a happy occasion. She could look back with justified satisfaction on her time in Mauritius and she could look forward with hope. She rejoiced at the number of young people in the eighteen to twenty-five age-group who had joined the Legion, finding in it a freedom and openness that was lacking in the older Catholic organisations. She had confidence in the commitment and ability of the Legion officers, especially young Father Margéot. Her confidence in him was not misplaced. He was to prove a pillar of strength to the Legion, first as spiritual director, then as vicar-general, then as Bishop of Port Louis, and finally as Mauritius's first Cardinal.

The boat was delayed and did not arrive until 13 September. Edel spent ten days in a kind of Limbo, meeting people she had said goodbye to and having to say goodbye again. They kept giving her more gifts, mainly of flowers and fruit. 'They are emotional too – the various mixtures, I suppose – and tears come a little easy, so it was a really cheerful ten days! The usual version was goodbye au ciel – we'll meet in heaven – this with eyes to heaven. Talk of strain – I thought the boat would never come.' Archbishop Leen gave her a generous gift of 510 rupees 'to go towards making the travelling as pleasant as possible' and asked her to pay a return visit in eighteen months. But she knew she would never see him or Mauritius again.

The voyage to Durban was a nightmare. The ship was unstable and the seas were rough. She was sick practically all the time. She crawled out of her bunk just half an hour before the ship put into Durban on 20 September 1940. As soon as it docked she found herself being taken in hand by the local Legion of Mary. 'At 2 p.m. I was in the boat, 3 p.m. Miss Keane was picked up, my coats and case packed, and at 3.30 p.m. I was sitting at a junior meeting at Maris Stella school here.' By the time she got to bed she was too tired to sleep so she wrote a midnight letter to John Nagle describing her voyage.

Tired though she was, she had not lost her sense of humour. In his last letter to her, John had commented on the extra money, £300 in all, that she had asked for in order to pay for her journeys. 'It is rumoured here,' he wrote, 'that you have eloped with the nice gentleman who presented you with the basket of flowers on your arrival in Mauritius and that you are blowing the £300 on your honeymoon!' In her reply, Edel defended the man with the flowers 'who is quite nice but a bit heavy on the uptake and he also has 9 or 8 children, though that is quite small in Mauritius.' She had finished the letter when she thought of an even more effective riposte. She added a devastating postscript, written like many of her postscripts in minute writing across the top of the page. 'By the way, speaking of honeymoons, do I remember anything of an evening in October '36 when a certain Miss Bodkin and a Mr Nagle were seen off in proper style at Euston?' It was game, set and match.

After a few days in Durban she was lucky enough to get a place on a boat for Beira in the Portuguese colony of Mozambique. She had another wait there as there were only two trains a week to Nyasaland, her next destination. A friendly priest she had met on the boat arranged for her to stay in a convent where the nuns spoke English and French. She left Beira at 7 p.m. on 30 September and travelled all through the night and the following day. It was 7 p.m. when she arrived at Limbé in Nyasaland. She breathed a sigh of relief. 'One of the priests here met the train and brought me to the convent, and wasn't I glad to get settled in somewhere. I had been travelling since 13 September to the evening of 1 October. This is good old Africa again, same type town, smallish, Indian shops, a town in the making.'

NINETEEN

Collapse

Edel had been travelling for nineteen days. For the first eight of these she had been more or less continuously sea-sick. She must have been very far from well when she arrived in Nyasaland, but she did not admit this to herself or to anyone else. All she would own to was a certain feeling of tiredness, only to be expected after her long journey. Now that she had arrived in Limbé and settled in at the convent, she was confident that she would soon be back to normal.

Nyasaland, now known as Malawi, was a long narrow country strung out along the southern and western shores of Lake Nyasa. It was a British protectorate and had a population at the time of a little less than two million. There were two Catholic Vicariates in the country and they cooperated closely on pastoral matters, with a common seminary and a common newspaper. The De Montfort Fathers were in the Vicariate of Shiré in the southern part of the country, the White Fathers in the Vicariate of Nyasa in the north.

Edel started in the south, where she felt sure of a welcome. The De Montfort Fathers had been founded by St Louis Marie de Montfort, whose teaching on the true devotion to the Blessed Virgin Mary was the foundation of the Legion's spirituality. She was certain of their sympathy with her aims and objectives. The Vicar, Bishop Louis Auneau, confirmed this when he met her. He told her he wanted the Legion established at all his missions and he would like the seminarians to be auxiliary members. 'He gave me a letter of introduction to all his priests (the first one I got since I came out!) which warmly emphasises his wish to see the Legion established.'

When she started her round of the missions, she found herself up against the familiar problem of transport. Her car was still in Dar-es-Salaam, separated from her by a thousand miles of bush roads and mountain tracks. The only car in the Vicariate was in constant use by the Bishop. All the other priests used motor-cycles. She tried for a while to hire cars but soon came to the opinion that it would be cheaper and more convenient to buy one. There was a Ford for sale in Limbé for £60 and one of the parishioners, an engineer, examined it for her. When he declared it to be in perfect mechanical condition, she decided to buy it and succeeded in getting it for £50. Then she wrote to Bishop Maranta in Dar-es-Salaam and asked him to sell the Rolls-Royce.

Her new driver was Joseph Cirikumwendo. Though a member of the Dutch Reformed Church, he later gave evidence for the canonisation process. He described how she used to spend much of the time on her journeys in prayer. Sometimes the roads were so bad that they had to abandon the car and walk. She would still pray as she walked along, reading from her book. Joseph did not know the name of the book, but it seems to have been the Little Office of Our Lady. She never complained about her health but he knew she must be sick because she coughed so much.

There were the usual difficulties to face in the missions she visited. In spite of the bishop's letter, not all of them welcomed her with open arms. A further problem was the wide variety of nationalities among the missionaries: French, English, Irish, Dutch, French-Canadian.

Here at some missions one speaks half English, half French - and what French! Today I was trying to remember some Swahili to tell the driver some things. Immediately after I had to speak to the Mother Provincial who only knows French, but I kept using Swahili for French words and was hardly able to make myself understood! Then you go a bit further and you meet a missionary who only speaks English as a second language and you have to remember to speak slowly etc. and to watch to know if he really understands what you have said.

She was still in Shiré when she heard the rumour about her death. No-one knows where it was started or by whom but it spread quickly through East Africa. It even reached Ireland though fortunately not her family. Edel was puzzled. 'If I had been even sick during the year,' she told John Nagle, 'I could have understood the exaggeration, but there was nothing to give ground for it, unless the fact that I was longer in Mauritius than I had expected.' On the whole she was rather amused, as she told Father Margéot in a letter to Mauritius.

By the way, I will tell you a good joke. Do you know when I was in Mauritius, the rumour got around here in Africa that I had died there! Requiem Masses were offered in various vicariates and headquarters got letters of condolence! I put the rumour down to the fact that Loreto Mauritius at Vacoas sent me soups and jellies to the hotel. They must have mentioned it to Loreto Nairobi, and Nairobi being Nairobi arranged the funeral. Several priests wrote me since, congratulating me on the Resurrection.

At the beginning of December she decided to move on to the northern vicariate. The rains were beginning and the roads in the south were turning into mud. Travel would be easier in the north, which had a number of all-weather roads. Besides, she had covered most of the missions in Shiré and could easily come back later when the rains were over to complete the work. Bishop Auneau gave her a parting gift of 'a very nice ivory paper knife and a small ebony box (which could do for powder or snuff!). I was very surprised as it is the first time I have ever got anything like than in Africa.' As Joseph did not want to go too far away from his home village, she found a new driver, Pancratius Cilakalaka.

The welcome she received from Bishop Oscar Julien in Nyasa Vicariate was even warmer than Bishop Auneau's. He had already held a meeting of mission superiors at which he told them of her coming and asked them to help her in her work. 'It is a dream in one way. Because the bishop is very keen on it and because the Delegate of the Pope wants it, they are all prepared to give it a chance, no matter what they think personally.' Her first impressions of Bishop Julien himself could hardly have been more favourable. 'The bishop is Canadian, very simple and very human.' Events were soon to show how well she had judged him.

Her base was the convent in Likuni mission, which was the bishop's residence. She was often away for several days at a time, including Christmas, which she spent at Mua. 'I am delighted to be here for Christmas as it is quieter than many missions and I do just as I please, appearing for meals.' It sounds just a little bit lonely. And indeed, for the previous few weeks thoughts of home had been in her mind, as she told Emma Bodkin.

You know, I arrived in this vicariate, White Fathers, on 8 December just shortly before evening Benediction. It suddenly struck me it was re-union Sunday at home and probably you were all at Benediction too. I was just a bit homesick for a gossip with all the crowd, the jokes, the remarks etc. One remembers it all so well. These special days. However, when the war is over, we can gossip. It would take an order to make me travel, even home, just at present. I am a coward on water – not like yourself, Emma!

She thanked Emma for all the prayers of all her friends in Ireland, especially those who took turns to pray for her, a day at a time. 'Sometimes, when something looking or working out all wrong suddenly turns out all right, I ask myself, Whose day is this for prayers? It is sometimes so obvious a change, one must query Why?'

After a brief Christmas rest she set off again, visiting and re-visiting the northern missions. She was beginning to flag but she pushed herself relentlessly. The pace proved too much for her driver, Pancratius, who complained of heart pains and resigned after only a month. 'I have another new driver. I should have kept count of all I had. This is at least the sixth – named Adam.' In a letter to John Nagle on 28 January 1941 she reported good progress in both of the Nyasaland vicariates. She planned to go back south to Bishop Auneau's territory to set up a Curia there and then to head off north again into Northern Rhodesia, where a number of vicariates or prefectures were awaiting her arrival.

She was probably already ill when she wrote that letter at the end of January, though she did not mention it. In February she went steadily downhill. In addition to the weakness and tiredness, she began to suffer severely from dysentery. This continued for fifteen days, during which she refused to go to bed and insisted on keeping all her appointments at the different missions throughout the Nyasa Vicariate. Eventually she met one of the White Fathers who had served as a medical chaplain during World War I. He dosed her with some kind of disinfectant, which cleared up the dysentery in twenty-four hours. Unfortunately, it was followed by an attack of malaria. She stayed in bed for a day or two until her temperature had returned to normal. Then she was on the road again, with her appointment book filled for the next three weeks.

The most important appointment was the setting up of the Curia in Shiré Vicariate. It was a long and tiring journey to Ngulundi, where the meeting was held. Bishop Auneau presided and the attendance included nine priests. Everything went well, the Curia was formally constituted, and a French priest, Father Delaunay, was appointed spiritual director. Edel was satisfied with the outcome, though she was now so weak that she could scarcely stand. She was persuaded to go to Limbé and was put to bed in the convent where she had spent her first night in Nyasaland. She diagnosed herself as suffering from pleurisy, an inflammation of the area around the lungs, often found in sufferers from tuberculosis.

She had been nearly a week in bed when she decided that she had better tell Frank Duff about her illness. She wrote to him on 28 February in rather shaky handwriting. She reminded him she had promised to let him know if ever she was ill. Now she was keeping her promise. She briefly recounted what happened over the previous few weeks and assured him that she was making good progress and was well looked after by the nuns. She blamed her illness in part on the food shortage in the northern vicariate. 'Here, however, it is a good climate and European food and lots of it.' The rest of the letter dealt with the new Curia and her plans for Northern Rhodesia. She ended, 'The sick information is only for G.H.Q. No word home, please, or to anyone else.'

She stayed on in the convent for another two weeks. Her progress was painfully slow. By the second week of March, she felt strong enough to get up for a little while and put on her clothes. She was worried about her family's reaction if they heard she was ill and she remembered how the photo taken near Limuru had set their fears at rest. As soon as she was able to stand, she had herself driven to a photographer's and had a number of pictures taken of herself. She sent copies of two of them home to her mother. 'I thought the snaps O.K. myself,' she commented later, 'though I was only barely able to stand when they were taken.' In actual fact, the photos were far from O.K. Though dimly lit and poorly focussed, they were clear enough to show how sick she was. Her face was grey and drawn and unsmiling, her eyes dull and lifeless. Her legs, where they could be

Edel in Nyasaland, recovering from illness.

seen below the hem of her long overcoat, were as thin as match-sticks and her shoes looked three sizes too big. It would be hard to imagine anything less likely to reassure her family.

A message came from Bishop Julien, who had heard she was ill. He invited her to come back to the convent in Likuni, where her room was ready for her and she could stay as long as she liked. Weak though she was, she accepted the invitation for certain reasons and prepared for the gruelling journey. The phrase 'for certain reasons' is her own. It is a strange phrase and untypical of her direct style. Evidently she did not want to spell out the reasons. One can only suppose that she felt she was more welcome in Likuni than in Limbé.

Before she left, Father Delaunay, the new Curia spiritual director, came to see her. He wanted to discuss some matters connected with the working of the Curia. In the middle of the conversation, he suddenly said to her, 'Do you realise you are dying?' He went on to ask her if she had made spiritual preparations for her death. It was only then that she admitted to herself how serious her condition was. As soon as she reached Likuni, she sent Frank Duff a telegram to prepare him for the worst. It arrived in Dublin on 15th March 1941 and it read, 'Private. Attack pleurisy over. See letter. Fairly weak. Weight seventy-five pounds. Impossible continue work presently. Considerable rest needed. Await instructions.' The letter she had written about her ill-health had not yet arrived.

For the next few weeks all that Dublin knew came from brief and cryptic telegrams. Each telegram was accompanied by a letter which gave fuller details, but did not arrive until long afterwards. They replied to her in the same unsatisfactory manner. 'Shocked by wire. Act as you think we would wish you to in circumstances. Should you come home?' They sent a second telegram to Ruby Roberts, the Legion of Mary envoy in South Africa, asking her to keep an eye on developments and go to Nyasaland if necessary.

The suggestion about coming home was the last thing Edel wanted to hear. Comfortably installed in Likuni convent, she was now inclined to take a more optimistic view of her situation. 'I am not feeling a bit like dying and I have developed an appetite which should put up the lost pounds. All here suggest a good rest of 6 weeks and then I should be all right and no need to go home (and be sunk on the way!).' She had a pleasant room, one which was reserved for sick priests or nuns, she was being well fed and had a nursing sister looking after her. In six weeks' time she would be ready to take on Northern Rhodesia.

On 25th March her temperature started to rise. The sister advised her to rest completely. She continued to get up for Mass every morning, but spent the rest of the day lying down or sitting in a chair. Her temperature went down for a few days then rose to 102 on 2nd and 3rd April. She and the sister looked at each other and said, 'Is it malaria?' It was. She had a quinine injection next morning, her temperature shot up to 105 and then down to 95 before it finally began to stabilise. In the space of two months, she had had dysentery, malaria, and pleurisy, followed by a second and more serious attack of malaria, all this combined with her general exhaustion and her underlying permanent condition of uncured tuberculosis.

Easter Sunday that year fell on 13th April. The following day, Bishop Julien had a serious talk with her. He told her that she would have to give up her work for some months. If she tried to keep going, she would end up having another relapse in some remote mission where there were no nursing facilities and the nearest doctor was a hundred miles away. 'Better see the doctor here and get his opinion,' he said, 'then you will be more satisfied.' She had avoided seeing a doctor all the past two months, perhaps fearing what the verdict might be. Now she was left with no escape.

The doctor examined me thoroughly and said a rest of six months, completely away from my work, was necessary with a change of climate. 'After four years in the tropics,' he said, 'some months in the sub-tropics would make all the difference.' He told me I'd have to put on at least a stone and a half to get back to normal and that, with good food, rest, and change of climate, would keep the old weakness from getting the upper hand. Otherwise, the result would be inevitable.

The food in South Africa, he also said, would be naturally a big improvement on what one could get in the bush. The latter was all right when one was well, but one needed more than that when convalescing. He suggested Johannesburg as high and dry and of course, with Miss Roberts there, it was convenient.

In face of all that, there was no alternative but to go south, so all was fixed up for 22nd inst. departure.

Bishop Julien appointed one of his priests to make the necessary travel arrangments. He found that it would be possible to take a plane for most of the journey and that the extra cost would be negligible. At the bishop's insistence, Edel agreed to the plane travel, her first time ever to fly.

She said goodbye to the bishop, whose kindness she would remember for the rest of her life, and to the sisters in Likuni. Then she set off on the long journey to Johannesburg, which was considerably shortened by the decision to fly. 'It meant 4 to 5 hours compared with at least 3 days, and if I did not go by plane it meant several hundred miles by car and one night in a rest-house, which amounts to camping out.' It was still a very tiring journey and she was utterly exhausted when she reached her destination.

The final stage was by train. Ruby Roberts went to the station in Johannesburg to meet her. Miss Roberts was fifty-seven years of age, a former schoolteacher who was now working as Legion envoy in the Union of South Africa. She was sturdily built, with the rimless glasses and severe hairstyle and brisk no-nonsense manner that fitted the traditional image of the schoolmistress. Appearances notwithstanding, she was to prove a very kind and faithful friend to Edel for the next two years.

Her first impression of Edel was of a radiant smile that seemed to belie the reports of her ill-health. It was only when she set off along the platform at her usual brisk pace and heard Edel panting along behind her that she realised how weak she was. She brought her to the place where she was staying herself, a hostel called Melrose House run by Dominican sisters. It was meant principally for business girls and was not ideal for a convalescent but it would do for the time being.

The superior of the hostel, Mother Angela, took one look at Edel and told her she must see a doctor at once. Edel was as usual reluctant so Mother Angela took matters into her own hands. 'They produced a doctor on me here and his verdict is to retire to a Newcastle again for a few months' treatment. He rejected all suggestions of staying elsewhere, at least for the present.' As there was no Catholic sanatorium in the vicinity, it was arranged that she should go to a government-run sanatorium not far from the city. It had at least one advantage: she would not have to pay for her treatment.

There was still the problem of her family, who as yet knew nothing of what was happening. Edel wrote home saying she had gone to South Africa for a rest and giving Melrose House as her address. She said nothing about her illness and told Legion headquarters to do the same. John Nagle wrote back and warned her that the secret could not be kept for ever.

It is quite possible that the information may reach them through some other channel and then both you and we would be placed in a very awkward position. You can well imagine how angry your people would be with us for having failed to notify them of your illness. Further, you will have to explain why you are in Johannesburg and what has brought you there. Both Mr Duff and I are of the opinion that you should write to your parents at once. Please let us know when you have done so.

The problem solved itself in a totally unexpected manner. The photographs of Edel taken in Limbé arrived in Monkstown and the family were aghast. They sent her an anguished letter full of such phrases as 'tired and worn out' and 'dying on your feet'. Mr Quinn wanted to contact Legion headquarters for information but Mrs Quinn dissuaded him, saying Edel would be annoyed. ('The family are well trained, you see!' she commented wryly.) It was just at this point that they received the letter from Edel saying she was in South Africa taking a rest. They were so pleased that they sent her a telegram telling her to enjoy her rest. Unaware of these developments, Frank Duff and John Nagle decided to visit the family and tell them of Edel's illness. It did not prove the ordeal they had expected. 'We were delighted to find that your mother and father and sisters took a most sensible and reasonable view of the matter. Your mother remarked that it was the mercy of God that you were not in Ireland during the past two winters, which were exceptionally severe, as it is doubtful if you would have survived them.' The Quinn family were appeased, at least for the moment.

TWENTY

Another Newcastle

The name of the sanatorium was Springkell and it was situated at North Rand, eleven miles from Johannesburg. Edel was admitted there at the end of May 1941. When they were registering her, they asked her date of birth and were amazed to find she was only thirty-four. They had thought she must be sixty years of age.

With the experience of Newcastle behind her, Edel can have had few illusions. She spoke of a few weeks' rest but she knew well that long months of inactivity lay ahead, the monotony broken only by tests and x-rays and experiments with the latest miracle drug. Worst of all was the loneliness. In Newcastle she had the comfort of visits from her family and friends. Now she was in a completely strange country with not a single friend except a woman she had met for the first time a few weeks ago.

In a letter to her father from Springkell, she wrote with unusual frankness about the stresses in her life. 'The most tiring part is that one is always with strangers. Even when the job of work is done, you have to meet them again at meals and recreation so it is a full day and one is really only able to relax in bed.' She was referring to her visits to different missions throughout Africa. But what she said applied with still greater force to the sanatorium, where even in bed she was in the company of strangers.

Ruby Roberts came out to see her every week and looked after any small errands that had to be done. She also organised members of the Legion of Mary in Johannesburg to visit her from time to time. Some of the sisters from Melrose House brought presents of fruit and cream, designed to fatten the invalid, and a cardigan and bed-jacket. Once a week a priest visited the hospital and brought Holy Communion to the patients. His visit was the highlight of her week.

The first couple of months were spent in eating and sleeping, while the colour crept back to her face and her weight almost imperceptibly increased. The doctors monitored her progress and gave her a full report on 16 July. She told Frank Duff all about it two days later.

I have been at this sanatorium six weeks now and according to the x-ray the old trouble on the left lung has reopened and there is a small cavity on the right. I saw the doctor in charge here two days ago for exact details of my condition. He told me about the x-ray result and said a very prolonged rest would be necessary and he did not think I could work in the tropics again. At present I was in the best place for climate and food. I asked if prolonged rest meant over twelve months and he said, 'At least'. So that is exactly how things stand. You can guess what it means not being able to work for the present, but if that is God's will one must say 'Fiat'.

Miss Roberts noticed how often the word *Fiat* was on her lips. It is a Latin word which means 'Let it be done'. It occurs many times in the gospels. '*Fiat voluntas tua*' in the Lord's prayer means 'Thy will be done'. Mary's reply to the angel Gabriel was, '*Fiat mihi secundum verbum tuum*', which means 'Let it be done to me according to your word'. For Edel the word *Fiat* meant total submission to God's will. She was offering herself in his service as unconditionally and unquestioningly as Mary did at the Annunciation. She believed absolutely that he would continue to protect her in the future as he had in the past. 'From the day I landed I have never been sick, had malaria or anything, that I wasn't in the best place for getting care and attention. There have always been doctors available, nursing sisters, etc., and no doctor has let me pay one penny for attendance. A missionary! It is just what one would expect on Our Lady's work. There is never anything to worry about.'

She was very touched when John Nagle told her that all the Dublin Legionaries were starting a novena of prayer to Blessed Louis Marie de Montfort for her complete recovery. 'It is expected that he will be canonised in the near future,' he wrote. 'Hence, we are expecting that he will do something big for you on this occasion.'

As her strength began to increase, so did her letter-writing. Her circle of correspondents was bigger than ever. She wrote regularly to Ireland, to the Legion, to her family, to her friends. She kept in touch with bishops and spiritual directors and Legion officers in Kenya, Uganda, Tanganyika, Mauritius and Nyasaland. She worried about the expense to the Legion of the two cars which now lay idle. The seminary in Nyasaland offered to buy one of them. 'I expect they will give a fair price,' she wrote, always the businesswoman. 'Of course, if they don't they won't get it.' They offered £35, which she accepted. Her mechanically-minded bishop in Dar-es-Salaam disposed of the other car for £30.

She made no complaints about conditions in the sanatorium to her visitors or correspondents. She took everything as it came. Her most constant visitor, Ruby Roberts, was less tolerant. She found the talk of some of the other women in the ward very offensive and said so to Edel. Her only answer was that they knew no better. It was something she had met before in Newcastle and managed to cope with. All the same, Miss Roberts felt that it must have been very trying for her. 'The atmosphere was horrible,' she said.

There was only one thing in Springkell that Edel found hard. That was the restriction on receiving Holy Communion. For her the Eucharist was her daily bread. On her journeys she would fast for long hours in the tropical heat, refusing even to drink a drop of water, so that she could receive Communion when she reached the next mission. To be deprived of this joy for six days out of every seven was the hardest cross she had to bear.

Miss Roberts was well aware of this. 'Going to Holy Communion seemed to be her greatest desire in this life,' she said. She began to make inquiries to see if there was a suitable Catholic hospital where Edel could go. Eventually she found one in a place called Umlamli in a mountainous part of Cape Province. It was a small mission hospital run by Dominican nuns which was intended for Africans but took European patients from time to time. It lacked the facilities of a city hospital but it did have a resident doctor. The high altitude and clear air made it suitable for a tuberculosis sufferer. Best of all, there was a chapel where Mass was offered every morning. Ruby used her influence with the local bishop and got Edel put on the waiting list.

She had been almost six months in Springkell when a vacancy at last occurred. The move took place on 14 November 1941. She left for Johannesburg in the morning, visited a dentist and had three teeth filled. At 8 p.m. she boarded the train with Ruby Roberts and travelled all night to Bloemfontein. They had breakfast there at 8 next morning and then took another train to Zastron, where they were met by the lady doctor and one of the priests. 'We drove right up into the mountains and there, in a regular horseshoe of hills, Umlamli nestles.'

She described the place in loving detail to her family. The hospital, a new building, was in the form of a hollow square enclosing a compound with a fountain and goldfish. She had a pleasant room to herself, its door opening on to the inner verandah, its windows looking out towards the valley. Dr Ditton, a Catholic in her thirties, was very kind and reputed to be very clever. The nuns looked after all the nursing themselves. She ended her letter with an almost audible sigh of contentment. 'There goes the Angelus. It seems to have a special sound out in the mountains. It is just lovely being back at a mission station again. I must write and thank the bishop in my Sunday-best writing.'

There was one disappointment. She was unable to attend Mass. Every day Mass was offered in the chapel, which was a couple of hundred yards from the hospital, up a slight incline. She found she was too weak to walk that short distance. There was talk of bringing her in a wheelchair but it came to nothing. It may be that the doctor felt it better that she should not go out into the cold so early in the morning. However, even if she could not be physically present she could hear the bell and join with the congregation in spirit and afterwards the priest brought her Holy Communion in her room every day. She felt herself enveloped in an atmosphere of prayer and faith, so blessedly different from Springkell and indeed from Newcastle.

The weeks passed quietly and uneventfully. Christmas came, bringing with it letters and cards and presents, among them a signed copy of a book by Archbishop Leen. Even more appreciated was a visit in January from Bishop Demont of Aliwal North, the local vicariate. Not only did he call to see her in her room, he also agreed to say Mass in the hospital sitting room so that she could attend. She was able to dress and walk to the sitting room for her first Mass in nine months. 'It was a treat to assist at Mass again. There was a second Mass immediately after the bishop's, so I really got two.'

As in Newcastle, the treatment was based on food, rest and fresh air. The medication consisted mainly of injections. In Springkell she had been getting injections of toxoid, a drug recently developed in South Africa, of which great things were hoped. Dr Ditton continued the toxoid treatment and added calcium injections. Her weight at the beginning of February was 90 lbs, an improvement on the 75 lbs of a year earlier, but still wretchedly low. The usual charge for European patients was £15 a month but Miss Roberts succeeded in getting it reduced to £7.

On 14 February 1942 she wrote her will. It was not a legal document, as it was signed only by herself, but it made her intentions clear. Any money she possessed belonged to the Legion of Mary and must be returned to them, together with her letters and papers. For her family and friends she had only a few personal keepsakes. 'Brooch and rosary to Leslie. Doll to Mums and crucifix. Black clock to Popa.' Frank Duff was to get her books, John Nagle an ivory knife, evidently the one she got from Bishop Auneau. 'Burial to be at Umlamli cemetery. Only tombstone to be a small wooden cross.'

As Easter approached the weather grew colder. The South African winter starts in March and can be very severe in a place like Umlamli, 6,000 feet above sea-level. She was moved to a large new room with a sheltered verandah and a stove for the winter. She had her meals in her room but spent the rest of the day on the verandah, lying on a stretcher. Dr Ditton was a camera enthusiast and her photographs, unlike Edel's, usually came out. She took two of Edel on her stretcher and they have been preserved. She looks more rested and at ease than in the unfortunate Limbé portrait. In one she is accompanied by two small African boys, in the other by two budgies.

The budgies were a constant source of interest and pleasure during her illness. In Springkell she had been part-owner of a budgie, Peter Toots, but she could not bring it with her when she left. A Legionary presented her with another one when she came to Umlamli and she named it, not very inventively, Tony Budgie. She was given a second one after Christmas which was not as handsome or as lively as Tony and she was not over-upset when it was eaten by the convent cat. Hearing of the bereavement, a friend sent her another one to which she gave the more imaginative name of Cleopatra, as a suitable mate for Anthony. A third arrived soon afterwards, called Tim, to complete what she called her family. One was blue, one white and one yellow, and their various escapades gave her material for her letters to her family.

July was mid-winter in Umlamli and the weather was bitterly cold. There was heavy frost every morning with biting winds and frequent falls of snow. The verandah was out of the question and even her room was chilly. The stove could not be used as it gave off

Edel in Umlami Hospital, 1942, with a young visitor and one of the budgies.

fumes which irritated her lungs. She spent much of the time huddled beneath the blankets, sometimes unable even to sit up and write letters. A portable radio given to her by some Johannesburg Legionaries proved a great boon. She had some scruples about accepting so valuable a gift but was reassured by Frank Duff: 'Not only did we approve of the gift of the wireless to you but we were very touched by the attitude it represented.'

She was now beginning to use a new means of communication called the airgraph. The correspondent wrote or typed the letter on a special form and returned it to the Post Office. It was then microfilmed and the roll of film, containing hundreds of letters, was flown to Europe. On arrival the film was developed and the letters were printed to approximately a quarter of the size of the original and sent to the addressees. This made writing home less tiring for Edel as she was restricted to a single page. Moreover, the airgraphs were delivered quickly and regularly, thus lessening the constant barrage of complaints from her mother. One of Edel's pre-airgraph letters to her began: 'My darling Mums, you will have my heart broken with your complaints about not getting letters. I have not time to write every week but certainly I write every two weeks. It is war-time and all letters cannot get through as long as ships are being sunk.' In fairness to Mrs Quinn it must be said that there was some basis for her complaints. Edel had not always told her the whole truth about her state of health. She admitted as much to her mother in a letter written in August.

That time was such a nightmare – one minute I was told a few months holiday and everything would be all right, then that it would have to be a longer rest, so I did not know where I was myself as regards anything for some time. Naturally I passed on things as I was told them and felt a fool afterwards. However, I am doing well now and that is all past. Some time when we get the chance of a talk I will explain it all.

The wintry weather showed no sign of improving. Edel began to get restless. She had put on another two or three pounds and had been allowed up for two concerts in the hospital. She felt that the worst was over. She decided to leave Umlamli, rather as she had decided to leave Newcastle, not because she was cured but because there was nothing more it could do for her. She wrote about her plans to Frank Duff, who was once again President of the Concilium as John Nagle had finished his six-year term.

> With Dr Ditton's full approval I am going up to Nairobi, Kenya. She agrees that the winter at Umlamli is too severe, especially as I would be up. This year they all say it was mild comparatively – and it was very severe for months and still is, and this year I spent it in bed. She thinks that as a change is necessary Nairobi is all right, particularly as it fits in as regards the Legion and it is as well to go there now as later and so save the extra moving. The main point is to get there soon before the summer heat makes the journey between Durban and Mombasa too severe. Therefore it is hoped I can get a boat before the end of October.

Dr Ditton gave her approval with reluctance. Ruby Roberts disapproved and said so. Frank Duff was far from happy. But Edel was determined. She found there was a boat expected in Durban on 15 October and she booked a passage for Mombasa. She practised walking in the convent garden to prepare for the journey. She found homes for her three budgies. The nuns washed her clothes and helped her with her packing. The priest fitted her radio with new batteries. After all the goodbyes had been said, the doctor drove her the forty miles to the station at Zastron on 14 October to begin her long journey to Nairobi.

She spent the night in Bloemfontein, then took another train next morning for Durban. She travelled all day and night and got to Durban at 8 a.m. on 16 October. After breakfast in the station she went to Cook's travel agency only to be informed that the voyage was cancelled. The ship had arrived as scheduled but had been taken over 'for other purposes', presumably for carrying troops. No further sailings to Mombasa were likely for several weeks.

At this low point salvation arrived in the shape of Ruby Roberts, who had come to say goodbye. She told Edel she was doing extension work for the Legion in Zululand, and she had an invitation for her to stay as long as she liked at the Benedictine mission hospital at Nongoma. The brother who had driven Ruby to Durban was returning to Nongoma next morning. Edel gladly accepted the invitation to go with him. She took two small cases with her, leaving the rest of her luggage in Durban.

They left the city at 8 a.m. for the two-hundred-mile drive. The first hundred miles went well. Then they hit mud on a steep hill, festooned with immobilised lorries. After two hours of pushing and pulling with the help of some bystanders, they turned the car, drove back thirty miles and took another longer route to Nongoma. It was the early hours of Sunday 18 October when she reached the mission. She had been travelling since the morning of the 14th.

It was an inauspicious start to what proved a very pleasant stay. The Benedictine sisters refused to take any payment as a mark of respect for the Legion. They provided her with a comfortable room

Edel with Ruby Roberts and little friends in Benedictine Hospital, Nongoma, Zululand, 1942.

close to the convent chapel, and she was able to attend daily Mass for the first time in eighteen months. The hospital had two doctors and a brand new x-ray machine. 'The result was quite good. It shows the right lung is healing quite nicely. It just takes time. The left was the same as always; it was the one always affected.'

Soon after her arrival, one of the priests took a photograph of herself and Ruby Roberts in the garden, accompanied by four Zulu boys. It is the last good photograph that we have of her. She sent her mother a copy with elaborate explanations. 'I look like a dying duck, as if I were too weak to get out of the chair. I was not going to send it at first, as you seem to get the wind up so easily but on second thoughts decided I would. I think the reason I look so strained is that the priest who was taking the snap took ages to pose us.' She looks exhausted rather than strained, still very thin and with her hair plentifully streaked with grey. One can understand the mistake they made in Springkell. She looks at least as old as Ruby Roberts, who was fifty-eight.

One of the doctors pressed her to stay on in Nongoma and she was tempted to do so. It had advantages over Umlamli: daily Mass, better medical facilities, a milder climate. But Nairobi continued to call. In Nairobi she would be at the centre of things, able to keep in touch with all the scattered outposts of her Legion empire. She promised that she would not do any more work than the doctors allowed.

Dr Ditton said I'd have to continue resting and that I could not undertake the ordinary active travelling daily life of an envoy. But correspondence and light Legion work was all right. The latter I interpreted as, say, a visit to form or open a Curia after arrangements had been made by others. The doctor here who looks after me whilst I am here said the same – 'A very quiet life, no travelling round like Miss Roberts does, no addressing big meetings. But correspondence and seeing people (I presume their seeing me and visiting) is all right.' The main thing is to continue building up strength and resting.

November passed and another South African summer began. Even if a ship became available in December, it would be unwise to risk the long haul along the east African coastline in the heat of summer. She made inquiries about air travel to Kenya and learned that there was a service from Salisbury to Nairobi. The overall cost of the journey was only 30 shillings more than the sea-voyage. She booked a seat for the flight on 11 January.

She accepted an invitation to spend Christmas in the Holy Rosary Convent at Edenvale, not far from Johannesburg. She took her leave of her hosts in Nongoma and arrived in Edenvale on 23 December. The community were all young and Irish, and Edel had friends and interests in common with them. She greatly enjoyed her week there, which started with a shopping spree on Christmas Eve. She attended midnight and morning Masses on Christmas Day and after an Irish-style Christmas dinner retired to bed to sleep it off. She was kept pleasantly occupied for the next few days with visitors to the convent, friends of the nuns and Legionaries from the neighbourhood.

Ruby Roberts came to Johannesburg on 31 December and Edel met her there. That night they set off together by train for Salisbury, the principal town of Southern Rhodesia. They stayed at the Dominican Convent in Salisbury and were joined there by a third Legion envoy, Ruby Dennison. She had previously served as envoy in South Africa and it was her request for assistance in 1936 that had brought Edel to Africa. After a period back in Ireland, Miss Dennison had been given a new assignment in the Belgian Congo. The only boat she could get brought her to Capetown and she was now on her way to her appointed territory. The three envoys held a summit meeting, comparing notes and sharing experiences and discussing plans for the coming year. Then they parted to their respective mission fields.

Edel left Salisbury at one o'clock on the afternoon of Monday 11 January 1943. As the little plane had to come down to refuel every three hours and did not fly at all after dark, the journey was very slow by modern standards. It was half past one on Wednesday afternoon when a grey and shaken Edel got off the plane at Nairobi aero-drome. 'I was airsick all the way except for one and a half hours,' she told her sister Leslie. 'Wasn't I glad to arrive!'

TWENTY-ONE

Better than All Books

Edel was met at Nairobi aerodrome by her old friend Captain Jack Byrne and driven to St Teresa's Convent in Eastleigh. Another old friend, Elizabeth Gannon, was there to greet her. Edel had stayed at Eastleigh from time to time in the past; now it was to become her permanent home. The Loreto Convent was no longer available, as it had been taken over by the government for the duration of the war.

She was given her usual room at the back of the little church, with the door opening directly on to the grounds. 'There are only three nuns, and they are busy all day at school and dispensary, so one can work, rest and do what one likes and no bother of talking to people. One can come and go and not worry.' When staying in the Loreto Convent, she often came home late and had to climb over the gate. In her present state of health, gate-climbing was no longer an option. She described her new home to her mother.

It is a convent for native work. The church is built on its own and at the end of the church are two rooms, one a sacristy, the other is meant for a priest. It is this room I have, very comfy, a built-in wardrobe, one specially built deck-chair with cushions which I have in and out of doors, and another fancy chair. Table for writing, press for books etc.

Quite near the church is a big open summerhouse with table etc. Here I spend all my day when I am at home. Eastleigh is the name of the convent. The summerhouse is delightful, cool in the hot weather. I have morning tea 10 a.m. and afternoon tea 4 p.m. here, as well as tea for visitors. The lunch and supper I have in my room and brekker in a dining room usually with whatever priest says Mass.

It was almost four years since she had last been in Nairobi. Her friends were shocked to see how much she had failed in the meantime. One of them described her as 'length without breadth'. She was painfully thin, her hair was greying, her voice was low, she seemed permanently out of breath. The bouts of coughing were more frequent and more harrowing. She was unable to walk more than a few yards at a time. Yet her eye was still bright, her sense of humour was unimpaired, her will was as strong as ever, even if her body could not longer respond as it did before.

Nairobi too had changed. It was now a city at war and its streets were full of soldiers and airmen in uniform. In 1940 Italy had entered the war as an ally of Germany. The northern part of Kenya bordered the Italian-held territories of Somalia and Abyssinia. Fighting broke out between the troops on either side, ending in victory for the British. Among the victims of the campaign were the Italian priests of Nyeri and Meru. Since their areas extended as far as the Italian border, they were regarded as a security risk. They were rounded up and interned and priests from other parts of Kenya had to try and fill the vacancies.

Archbishop Riberi was another victim. As an Italian, he was considered unacceptable as Apostolic Delegate. He was protected by diplomatic immunity and was allowed to go back to Italy. The Delegation was moved from Mombasa to Nairobi and the duties of the Delegate were taken over temporarily by Edel's friend Father J. J. McCarthy, who had fortified her with tea and ham sandwiches in Dar-es-Salaam. Another of Edel's priest friends, Father John Reidy, had been appointed to the mission on the island of Zanzibar, the furthest outpost of the vicariate. Father Tom Maher was now an army chaplain, and wore the uniform of a British army major; he was still stationed in Nairobi, a reassuring link with the past.

Bishop Heffernan came to see her the day after her arrival, which pleased her greatly. He continued to visit her regularly, as did many of her friends. They brought presents of sweets and fruit and invalid foods until the cupboard in her room was filled to overflowing. 'I take three glasses of milk a day and two raw eggs – not bad for me!' She was given invitations to outings and dinners, most of which she gracefully declined. She was determined to husband her strength and avoid any journeys outside Nairobi.

This still left her with plenty of work. Her correspondence continued on its usual epic scale, all of it written by hand as her Baby Empire was in Durban with the rest of her luggage. She visited meetings of Curiae and Praesidia in the Nairobi area. A bus passed the convent regularly and took her the three miles into the city; someone usually gave her a lift home. A British serviceman, Joe Ibbett, who had been a Legionary in England, proved a great support. He accompanied her to many meetings and did a lot of the talking for her, helping to conserve her voice.

Some of the Legionaries in Ireland who had been praying for her began to say that she had been miraculously cured. A telegram arrived from Father Creedon, a priest prominent in the Legion in Dublin, whose piety was not always tempered by common sense. It read, 'Congratulations on splendid recovery.' She was afraid that the Legion journal *Maria Legionis* would print the rumour and she wrote at once to Frank Duff, 'Will you see that nothing gets in about a recovery.' She was equally firm with her mother, leaving her no room for false hopes.

> I am just as I was re the lungs. Either at home or abroad these things do not heal fully and the most one can hope for is to keep fairly well by eating and going easy. But the fact that I am up and about and able to go places doesn't mean a sudden cure. I'd have been able to do the same twelve months ago if they let me. I do say, of course, that all the prayers must have an effect to keep me as well as I am, otherwise I could not do what I am doing. But one must have faith and if God wants one to be well enough to do a certain amount, He'll arrange it, and if He doesn't, then it is His will – why worry?

She had been in Nairobi for over a month before she managed a visit to the Carmelite Convent. In 1938 four Carmelite sisters had come from Hampton Convent in Dublin at Bishop Heffernan's invitation to set up a foundation in Kenya. After some vicissitudes they were now settled in a new convent in Nairobi, the first contemplative order in Kenya. Edel had met them a number of times in 1939 but had not seen their new convent. Apart from her attraction to the contemplative life, Edel had a special interest in this convent as her friend Emma Bodkin had two sisters in the Hampton community.

She sent Emma an account of her visit and her meeting with the prioress, Mother Dympna. 'Unfortunately there were a few other visitors but Mother Dympna managed a fair chat. They seem ever so happy and she was so glad to have heard from you for Christmas. They have an ideal spot and through the window I caught a glimpse of their garden, which as Mother says does not look new.'

It was about this time that Edel had another bout of malaria. 'Just the usual: temperature for a few days, took atebrin, came down. Of course, that always bowls one over for a bit, for the week or so it and its effects last. It is more weakening than any other temperature somehow.' Seeing her condition, Bishop Heffernan asked Mother Dympna to let her come to the convent for a few weeks' convalescence. Mother Dympna was agreeable and she invited Edel to spend Lent and Easter with the sisters, living inside the enclosure and sharing in the life of the community.

Nothing could have come as a greater surprise to her or given her more joy. Her first choice of a calling had been that of a contemplative nun and she still felt drawn to that life as strongly as ever. In her more optimistic moments, she dreamed of a time when she had finished her work as an envoy and could join the Carmelite community in Nairobi. Now she was to have the opportunity of living that life and experiencing that vocation from the inside. It was an unheard-of privilege, as the Carmelites were a strictly enclosed order, but the bishop had given his permission, asking only that complete secrecy be observed.

Edel told nobody in Ireland about the invitation except Emma Bodkin, though she gave Emma permission to tell Frank Duff and 'the Gang' in strict confidence. To her family she merely said she was going to another convent for a few weeks' rest: 'to avoid visitors one has to clear right away.' In Eastleigh callers could walk into her room any hour of the day or night and she found it hard to cope with them in her weakened condition. The day before she left for the Carmelite convent was busier than ever.

I had one visitor after the other from 2 p.m. till 9 p.m. The joke about the last one was, he was a soldier whose people I had met in Salisbury. He got my address, missed one bus and got the 7 p.m. There was no other one back till 9 p.m. so I entertained him from under my mosquito net in bed. Luckily I had been warned that if you let him ramble about his girls etc. it was O.K. So I got him on to that. It was too late to offer him a meal, the sisters having finished supper, so I fed him on sweets someone had given me.

The next day the bishop collected her at Eastleigh and drove her to the Carmelites. She was completely exhausted when she arrived. The nuns installed her in the infirmary, a room on the first floor where she would have privacy and peace. In obedience to her doctor's orders, she spent the first three days in bed. Then she started to feel a little stronger and gradually worked out a daily timetable which allowed for prayer and work as well as rest.

She got up each morning for Mass in the convent chapel. She went back to the infirmary and rested for a while after breakfast. If she felt fit enough, she joined the sisters for their recreation after lunch. In the afternoon, she took another period of rest in her room or in the garden. One of the priests brought over her deck-chair from Eastleigh and she would sometimes sit in a sheltered corner and read or write. She usually took part in the sisters' evening recreation and they found her a cheerful and light-hearted companion. After supper she returned to the infirmary for the night and often spent some more time writing letters. How long, nobody knew.

Nor did they know how much time she spent in prayer. They often saw her in the chapel during the day, kneeling or sitting in the presence of the Blessed Sacrament. They did not doubt that she prayed at other times as well. She never spoke to them about her own spiritual life, but they were conscious of it all the time. 'Whenever you came into her presence,' one of them testified, 'whether it was in the infirmary or in the alcove where she used to sit, it was like entering a sanctuary, there was peace all around and you could feel her holiness.'

This did not prevent her from enjoying the high spirits of the younger sisters and the occasional practical jokes they played on her. On her very first night there, two of them came into the dimly lit infirmary and pretended they were American nuns who had come to visit the Legion of Mary envoy. When she started to worry that her secret had got out, they could not keep up the pretence any longer. They burst into laughter and she joined in.

She was hardly in a position to retaliate in kind, but her sense of humour still flashed out from time to time. One day she was in the infirmary for an afternoon siesta and she called out to the infirmarian, 'Mother, I can't sleep. Could you get me Dr Leen's book about the Holy Ghost? It always puts me to sleep in a couple of minutes.'

When Holy Week came around, she jotted down some of the thoughts that came to her during this solemn season. She was to do the same thing three or four times during the months that followed. These notes were found among her papers after her death and they are the only authentic record we have of her interior life.

Among them are some reflections on Mary and the Eucharist, two central themes of her spirituality. These were probably written on Holy Thursday, the day that commemorates the institution of the Eucharist at the Last Supper. Two of the sisters recalled afterwards how she had spent most of that day in the chapel, praying in front of the Altar of Repose. One of them walked in on her unexpectedly. 'As soon as I opened the door, she looked me and her face was radiant with joy. She seemed so happy and so much at ease in front of the Blessed Sacrament.' The other did not dare to come in and look after the candles for fear of disturbing her. Edel's notes, disjointed though they are, may convey something of the richness of that day's experience.

All today Mary loves Jesus in me, caresses and compassionates Him for all His wounds. But above all else she thanks Him for the Eucharist, and the Eternal Father for this gift. How lonely life would be without it! Thank the Trinity over and over again for this gift.

Keep Our Lord company in the Blessed Sacrament. The disciples asked, 'Where dwellest Thou?' They abode with him all day.

In dryness, just stay with Him. Mary will love and adore. 'It is good for us to be here', even if attention wanders, like a child with its mother.

Our very presence tells Jesus we love Him, even if we are too stupid and too earthly-minded to appreciate and behave properly in His presence. Offer Him through Mary to the Trinity in thanksgiving, love and adoration.

We want to be united with Him, to give ourselves to Him utterly. Our faith tells us He is in the Eucharist: let us seek Him there. If we knew we could find Him anywhere on earth, we would try to go there. We have Him, every free moment, on the altar. Be with Him there, better than all books.

Edel's stay with the Carmelites came to an end on Easter Tuesday and she returned to Eastleigh. 'It was a wonderful privilege and a wonderful rest,' she told Emma Bodkin, 'and they spoiled me in every possible way as well as feeding me in style.' She felt so much better after her combination of retreat, holiday and rest-cure, that she started planning journeys outside Nairobi. On 17 May 1943, just three weeks after her return, she sent Frank Duff an airgraph telling him of her intentions.

I leave tomorrow to visit the South Nyeri Curia. It meets about 80 miles from here. I am going there now to avoid the rains in June and July. The Spiritual Director told me he thought of dividing the Curia but would like to see me first. I do not think there is any need to divide. I shall be back in about ten days as I can visit some Praesidia as well.

This is a 'trial' run, so to speak! I am taking things easy otherwise. Because I make this trip, don't think I am able for a lot. I am not pretending I am. There is a good deal to be done, even here in Nairobi.

She spent from 18 May to 2 June in the Vicariate of Nyeri. This was the Vicariate which she had gone to four years earlier at the invitation of Bishop Re, only to fail as a result of the priests' lack of interest. Much had happened since then. All the Italian priests of Nyeri had been interned as enemy aliens and their place had been taken by Irish priests from Bishop Heffernan's Vicariate. As a result, the Legion of Mary had been introduced and most of the missions now had Praesidia.

She took a native bus for the eighty-mile journey from Nairobi. Once arrived at her destination, the priests drove her from one mission to another. In the course of two weeks she dealt with the Curia question (she agreed to the division), visited five missions and attended seventeen Legion meetings. Apart from her inability to walk any distance, she found that she could cope with all the demands made on her. The one thing she found trying was being fussed over, as she told her mother.

You'd laugh at meetings. The priests all know I have been ill and chase round after me with cushions, produce deck-chairs when we get back to the mission, and lay down the law if I don't eat lots. Of course, nothing is so calculated to send me clean daft as being fussed over and it takes me all my time not to blow up.

I did the other day. I had been a few days at the mission and the priest had fussed and at meals produced raw eggs and milk etc. When it came to dinner I left half the soup and he started fussing. Without thinking I said, 'Father, you are a very rude host!' It stopped him all right, but I was sorry as he got very red and apologised. I had only met him for the first time two days before. I apologised myself before I left but he told me I was right. As you'd say, I always think I am! However, we are quite good friends in spite of it. But it does make you mad.

A pattern established itself over the next few months. Many of her days were spent at Eastleigh, writing letters in the summerhouse. She had by now become a kind of clearing house for the Legion in Africa, maintaining communications between Dublin and the many areas in which she had worked. Some of her letters concern her two fellow envoys. Ruby Dennison, enthusiastic but erratic, had a habit of turning up in any place except the one assigned to her; it became Edel's responsibility to keep track of her movements. Ruby Roberts, solid and dependable, had just been given Egypt as her new field of operation and Edel was using her Nairobi contacts to get her the necessary travel documents.

She continued her regular visits to the Curiae and Praesidia in the city and its environs; these included a new Forces Praesidium for members of the armed services. She undertook the task of setting up a Comitium, a kind of super-Curia which would co-ordinate the work of the native and non-native Curiae in Nairobi. It was a task fraught with racial problems, and she was not surprised when one of the European Legionaries expressed doubts about allowing Africans to be members: 'this colour question comes into everything.' At the same time, she had to deal with a kind of reverse racism on the part of some of the priests. 'It is difficult to explain, but most priests who take up native work consider it part of the latter to keep as far away from non-natives as possible and in a measure to despise (I wonder if that is the right word?) them, or at least affect to do so. To say the least of it, it is a most unchristian attitude.' In spite of all the obstacles, the Comitium came into being.

Buoyed up by the success of her Nyeri expedition, she began to extend her trips, sometimes for a day, sometimes for two or three days at a time. It was on one of these trips that she met Bishop Shanahan, the great Nigerian missionary, now living in retirement at Kalimoni mission. He was very ill and, though he joined her and the priest in charge for a meal, he was unable to speak more than a few words to her.

On these journeys she was once again dependent on others for transport, using cars and trains and native buses or taxis. One of her letters describes a typical bus journey.

Last week I was going to visit a mission about 70 miles from here. Left Eastleigh, where I stay, at 7 a.m. after brekker. Local bus to a nearby petrol station. Sat there on wall for 1 hour with my attache case till native taxi [bus] arrived. Full up. After talk – it is the usual one I take – they squeeze a place. The bus is divided up. One seat in front with driver, 1st class. A seat across behind this, cut off from rest of bus, is 2nd class. Here they got me in, it holds five. We had two Indian men and two women, a few kids, under seat three chickens.

One of the women was sick all the way and the bus had to stop for her every now and then. Luckily I was at the window and don't get car-sick, but by the time we had done over 50 miles I was feeling squeamy, particularly when one of the kids got sick. Then, just two miles from where the car was meeting me, a puncture. Luckily they had a spare. We got out for half an hour. The sick woman got out, got her family together, produced food and tucked in in great style as if never sick! We went on, the local chief's car, driven by his son, met me. I got to the mission.

One thing she does not mention, because it was taken for granted, is the dust. In the dry season the untarred roads were covered with layers of dust. When the bus passed another vehicle, thick clouds of dust billowed in through the glassless windows and choked the passengers. It was trying enough for the normal person. For someone who found it hard to breathe under the best of conditions it must have been devastating. She did not complain.

She undertook a longer tour at the end of September to set up Curiae in the Vicariate of Kilimanjaro. An overnight train from Nairobi brought her to Bura, where she rested for a day and a night. Then she went on by car to Kilimanjaro, visiting missions on the way. She stayed for three nights at Kilema, where she had slept on the veranda six years earlier. They now had eighteen thousand Christians and four African priests. 'It was fine on Sunday to hear them preach and say Mass (actually I did not appreciate the sermon too much as it was for 30 minutes). I met the bishop here and he asked me if I meant to die fighting!'

Bishop Byrne's remark was a none too subtle reference to her appearance, which shocked all who remembered her from her earlier visits. Among them was Sister Angelita, who had moved from Kilema to the convent in Kibosho. 'She was very weak at that time,' she recalled; 'she couldn't walk more than eight or ten steps without stopping to get her breath back.' When the sisters at Kibosho saw Edel to her bedroom, they advised her to lock her door for reasons of security. Edel asked them to lock the door from the outside and take the key away. She was afraid she would cause them inconvenience if she was unable to get up in the morning and unlock it herself.

Transport had been the great problem on her previous visit. This time it was no better. 'One depended on a chance lorry going the way one wanted the day one wanted.' In spite of the difficulties, she succeeded in getting three Curiae established. Things were made easier for the last week when one of the mission superiors lent her his car and his assistant priest as driver. 'It is a very generous gesture as it means he has to walk to and from an out-station for the week-end Mass and get another priest to take his place here who cannot walk so well. I must say that when one is not too strong one gets a lot more help than if one is independent.'

She was back in Nairobi at the beginning of November, having spent a week in Bura on the way. She did not rest on her return; the next few weeks were as busy as ever, with letters and meetings and travel. 'I shall be at Thika Curia tomorrow,' she wrote on 19 November, 'go on to Nyeri Vicariate for their Curia and Comitium next week, so I won't be back in Nairobi till 28th inst. Therefore excuse no letters being written till then.'

She wrote to Frank Duff on 2 December after her return. While she did not admit to being tired, she was evidently looking forward to a rest. Her letter ended: 'I shall take it easy for a few weeks round Christmas and try to get my mail off or down! The form keeps good, no fever, sleep like a top. Can't you pray me more walking power?' The few weeks' rest she was looking forward to was a return visit to the Carmelite Convent.

TWENTY-TWO

Death in Africa

Edel's last Christmas holiday began on 23 December 1943. The weeks leading up to Christmas had not been easy. There were various problems in Legion circles in Nairobi, including a dispute about a social club being run for servicemen. Another source of worry was Father Culligan, a committed but over-zealous spiritual director who insisted on the Legionaries attending retreats and study circles in addition to their normal commitments. Edel went to one of his day retreats for the sake of peace, though it was raining heavily, and caught a severe cold as a result.

When she arrived in the Carmelite Convent two days before Christmas, she seemed weak and depressed. The nuns noticed particularly the colour of her lips. 'They were a strange purplish colour,' one of them said, 'almost as if they were dyed.' She was given her old room, the convent infirmary, and told to rest. Her only exertion on Christmas Eve was to join in the ritual stirring of the plum pudding before it was cooked. On Christmas Day the nuns heard the news of the death of Bishop Shanahan who had been their chaplain until his health failed. The following day Edel was among the large crowd who attended his funeral. She brought back a full description to the nuns, who were not permitted to leave their enclosure.

For the rest of her stay she did her best to take things as easy as possible. At the same time, she was anxious to cause no trouble to the sisters. She reminded the infirmarian to make sure that any tableware she used was thoroughly sterilised to avoid the risk of infecting others. One night she had a heart attack but did not ring her bell for help. The infirmarian only found out about it the next morning when she asked Edel how she had slept.

The thought that she might die in the convent seemed to cause her considerable anxiety. She was not thinking of herself but of the worry and disruption that this would entail for the sisters. It would

also mean that people would come to know that she been staying inside the enclosure, causing embarrassment to Bishop Heffernan and
to the community. She told one of the nuns she was praying to Our
Lady not to let her die in the convent.

She left on the 11 January 1944 and returned to her room in
Eastleigh. She always described the place in glowing terms in her
letters, but the accounts given by her friends were less enthusiastic.
The room was very small, with hardly any space for all her books
and files. The nuns used it for washing the altar linen and she had to
leave it on these occasions. The fact that it opened directly on to the
grounds put her completely at the mercy of visitors. One afternoon
while she was trying to have a siesta a hen came in and laid an egg
on the bed at her feet. She told this as a joke, but it underlines the
lack of privacy. Other disadvantages were the distance from the city
and the personality of Mother Arsenia, the superior, who was said to
be difficult to get on with. Edel got on with her very well, but it must
have been yet another source of strain.

Worries continued to mount up. They were not all that serious
and she could have coped with them easily in days gone by. Now
she found that she was tired all the time and even the simplest task
demanded an almost superhuman effort. Somehow or other she
made the effort. The letters written during these last months of her
life are as clear and organised as ever. Her luggage arrived from
Durban in January and she used her beloved Baby Empire for some
of these letters. But even those written by hand show no sign of fail-
ing strength.

Her main problem concerned the club being run by the Forces'
Praesidium in Nairobi. It was intended for servicemen and met in
the parish rooms every Wednesday and Saturday from 7 to 11.15
p.m. The men played cards and other games, had some music and
singing, and were given a snack supper. Once a month a dance was
held. All was going well until the priest in charge of the parish
started taking over the club and putting his own nominees on the
committee. He wanted to use the club partly as a means of raising

funds for a planned new cathedral, which was against the Legion
rule. Edel wrote to John Nagle at great length about the dispute.
When she had filled one airgraph she started on a second and then a
third. Her decision, which he approved, was for the Legion to with-
draw from the running of the club and to concentrate on the new social centre which Bishop Heffernan had asked them to build.

The idea of the centre came up because a meeting place was
needed for members of inter-church marriages, of which there were
many among the European community in Nairobi.

The putting up of a Social Centre was decided on and the bishop
gave a site on the church grounds. Welfare (Military) are to give
a grant and a loan, as it is also to be open to European members of
the Forces. The latter are forbidden to mix with Goans. The matter has been going through various channels, so many commit-
tees and controls have to approve of everything nowadays. The
building is for the duration of the war and probably for some time
after. Then at His Lordship's express wish the funds that may ac-
crue plus the value of the building at the end of the period are to
go to building a permanent Legion centre in Nairobi.

She apologised to her mother for a gap in her correspondence,
caused by the new venture. 'All sorts of people had to be seen for
permission, priests, bishop, local authorities, and then a plan finally
got out. The few of us on the job had a rush. We hope to know at the
end of the week if it can go up. Then the work will really begin – but
it won't be my affair directly, D.G.' In a post-script she adds, 'I have
got to get a hair-set as it is long overdue. My hair is dreadful. One
has to wait weeks for an appointment.'

By the middle of February she was planning a return visit to the
Vicariate of Kisumu to see the Praesidia she had set up in 1938 and
to organise Curiae. She told Frank Duff that she would leave on 8
March and spend about five weeks there. 'I think too,' she went on,
'it will be no harm if I leave Nairobi for a while; if one is there, Legionaries are rather inclined not to decide anything for themselves

without first asking me.' Later in the year she intended to go to Dar-es-Salaam, when June and July brought some cooler weather to the coast.

From one point of view, the decision to go to Kisumu was an act of supreme folly. She was weak, tired and ill. Her voice was almost gone. She could not walk more than a few steps at a time. By having recourse to the old reliables of rest, fresh air and healthy food, she could hope to prolong her life for perhaps a few more months. By going on a long and tiring and stressful journey, she was certainly hastening her death. Any of her friends would have told her this if she had asked them for advice. She did not ask them. She had no advisers. She had no regular doctor. She had confessors but no spiritual director. Her obedience was to the Concilium and to the voice of her conscience. The Concilium were far away and they confined themselves to general exhortations about acting prudently and not over-taxing her strength. Her conscience said: Go.

Among the questions asked of all those who gave evidence at the canonisation process were a number about her attitude towards her health. Did she endanger her health? Did she do so rashly? Did she conceal her ill health? If so, what was her motive? Whom did she regard as her superiors in this respect? What was her attitude to them in this matter? Most of the witnesses found these questions hard to answer. They could scarcely deny that she did her best to conceal her ill-health and that she constantly pushed herself to the limits. Yet they felt that the ordinary rules did not seem to apply to her. 'We couldn't get her to rest as long as there was work to be done,' said Mother Philip Silver, who met her on this last visit to Kisumu. 'As members of a religious congregation, we felt we had the duty to our congregation of looking after our health, but she hadn't.'

From the moment she set foot in Africa, her attitude had been consistent. She knew she had a limited time to live and she was determined to use every minute of that time. She never saw prolonging her life as an end in itself. What mattered was not the length of life but the way she lived it. She did not take needless risks. When she was ordered to rest by the Concilium or by the local bishop or by the doctors in the various sanatoria, she obeyed. But the purpose of resting was not to buy a few more months of inactivity. It was to give her the strength to continue her mission. She must work while the light lasted. The night was coming when no-one could work.

On 8th March Elizabeth Gannon drove her to Limuru to catch the train for Kisumu. After an exhausting all-night journey she arrived at her destination on the morning of the 9th. She went to see Bishop Stam and was glad to find him still a firm supporter of the Legion. 'I hear that when he makes his visitation at a mission he always asks about the Legion and where possible insists on seeing them and asks exactly what they are doing and what results they have got.' By a happy coincidence, all the priests whose missions she intended to visit happened to be in Kisumu when she arrived and she was able to complete the plans for her itinerary with them.

It was five years since her previous visit to the Vicariate and she was interested to see how the Legion had fared in the meantime. She found, as she expected, that it fared best when the spiritual director went regularly to meetings. The native Praesidium in Kisumu had lapsed because the priest was unable to attend. She reassembled as many as she could find of the original members and got it going again. On the other hand, the non-native Praesidium was still meeting and working away though the priest never attended; indeed, he was not even aware of its existence.

She became more convinced than ever of the importance of a strong Curia in each district which would give support to the individual Praesidia. The Curia at Mumias was working well but it covered only one area of the vicariate. She decided that two more Curiae were needed, one at Rangala and the other at Kakamega. She started with Rangala.

Setting up a Curia was something she had done many times before. This time it was different. The weather was hot and damp and sticky. Visiting the different missions and Praesidia that would fall under the new Curia drained her of her last reserves. The priests were very sympathetic and drove her wherever she wanted to go. She even had to be driven the few yards from the convent to the priest's house in Rangala. But finally the work was done and she was able to inform Dublin officially of the founding of a new Curia. It was her last.

The Curia just started is the Rangala-Abaga District Curia, meeting place Rangala and Abaga alternately every two months. Spiritual Director, Rev. Fr. Van den Bosch, Catholic Mission, P.O. Yala, Kenya; President, Bro. Athanasi Ranganya, same address; V.P. Bernardine Omkigwa; Secretary, Bro. Romulus Omolo; Treasurer, Dalmas Akwoyo. There are five attached Praesidia. I shall send you a form as well by surface mail. This Curia is in the Kisumu Vicariate and the language is Luo.

Kakamega should have been next on her list but it was apparent to everyone, even Edel, that she could go on no longer. Father van den Bosch put her in his car together with Sister Peter, who was a nurse. He drove her to Kisumu town and deposited her in the Franciscan convent at Kibuye. 'Put her to bed and keep her there,' he said before driving back to Rangala. The sisters remembered with sadness the blithe young woman who had leapt from her taxi in the self-same spot six years ago and introduced herself. 'My name is Edel Quinn and I think you are expecting me. Am I in time for Mass or can I get Holy Communion?'

Edel was down but not quite out. She could still write. She got in touch with Miss Dickson, a schoolteacher who was President of the Comitium in Nairobi and had some of her holidays left. Miss Dickson agreed to come up to Kisumu and take on the job of forming a Curia in Kakamega.

She wrote to her family and to Frank Duff and John Nagle, making no mention of her condition. She wrote letters of thanks, as was her custom, to all the priests and nuns who had offered her help and hospitality during the previous few weeks. Among them was Sister Peter, who had left her a bottle of cough medicine. 'I am only using it when absolutely necessary, it is so precious and effective.'

She delayed her return to Nairobi, partly to recover her strength, partly so that she could meet Ruby Roberts again. Thanks largely to Edel's efforts, Ruby was now on her way to Egypt. Her plane was due to land at Kisumu airport en route and Edel looked forward very much to meeting her again. The plane was delayed and Edel had to wait five hours at the airport gate in the blazing sun, sitting on a chair someone had provided for her. It was to end in disappointment, as she related to Frank Duff.

I did not see her on the way up because she had only a break of half an hour at Kisumu, where they do not leave the airport, and unless one has been inoculated for yellow fever one cannot get in. She was to have been motored to the gate of the airport to meet me, but the airways agent got a special call at the last moment so it did not come off. However I was in Kisumu at the time so it did not mean an extra trip. They have a night stop at Kampala, but that was too far away to go to.

Edel felt the disappointment very keenly. Over the years her respect and indeed love for Ruby Roberts had grown steadily. Beneath the rather forbidding exterior, she had come to see Ruby's real qualities, her courage, her integrity, her dedication, her warmth of heart. 'She has really been kindness itself to me,' Edel had written from her Johannesburg sanatorium, 'and no-one could go to more trouble to look after me and see to things, arrange for visitors, etc. etc. She seems like one of the family, the care she takes of me, and nothing is too much trouble for her.' In those dark days, Ruby had taken the place of a mother for her. Now she would never see her again.

Easter Sunday fell on 9 April in 1944. Two days later Edel returned to Nairobi by train from Kisumu. She was met at the station by Elisabeth Gannon's sister, Mrs Máire O'Shea, who brought her back to her own comfortable home for a few hours. Edel rested on a couch in front of the fire and drank tea and talked about her family.

In the afternoon Mrs O'Shea drove her back for the last time to her little room behind the church in Eastleigh.

Edel was tired in a way she had never felt before. It was a tiredness that seemed to reach down into the depths of her being. For the remaining month of her life she never left the convent. Her time was spent between her room and the summerhouse in the garden a short distance away. The morning was spent in bed. Because of the wartime shortage of priests, Mass was not said every morning in the church. When it was, she could hear the priest through the thin partition wall and join in the prayers. After Mass, she would receive Holy Communion in her room.

In the afternoon she went to the summerhouse, where there was a comfortable chair and a table. There was a regular flow of visitors, who found her cheerful though painfully weak. She often dealt with her correspondence in the summerhouse, reading and writing almost up to the end. She stopped using the Baby Empire, perhaps because she lacked the strength to strike the keys, but her handwriting remained firm and legible.

Elizabeth Gannon came to see her every evening after work to prepare her for the night. Edel looked forward to her visit. The nuns were willing to help her but she insisted on waiting for Miss Gannon. The night that followed was long and restless. Mother Arsenia, coming to the church shortly after five o'clock in the morning, would see the light on in her room and hear the sound of coughing. She never spoke about this or made any complaint and she refused to let the nuns call a doctor to see her.

Her last surviving letter was written to Frank Duff on 9 May, three days before her death. It is a long and business-like document, dealing with a wide range of topics all over Africa, Ruby Roberts in Egypt, Ruby Denison no-one knew exactly where, a projected extension of the Legion to the Sudan, a girls' hostel planned for Durban, Holy Rosary Sisters going to Nyasaland. She also referred to events in Dublin, Frank Duff's new hearing aid and his continuing troubles with Archbishop McQuaid. She spoke only briefly of her health. 'I am still paying for my Kisumu trip and Curia. It proved too much for me.' She mentioned that she was going up to 'Emma's friend' for some weeks towards the end of the month. Emma's friend was the Prioress of the Carmelite Convent.

She kept a carbon copy of this letter in her files. On the blank space at the end she wrote out a prayer, possibly copied from a book. It may be the last thing she ever wrote.

Holy Mary, Mother of God and Virgin, I choose thee this day for my Queen, Patron and Advocate, and firmly resolve and purpose never to abandon thee, never to say or do anything against thee, nor to permit that aught be done by others to dishonour thee. Receive me then, I conjure thee, as thy perpetual servant, assist me in all my actions, and do not abandon me in the hour of my death. Amen.

The following afternoon Father Culligan visited her and found her in the summerhouse. She looked weaker, her skin yellower, her eyes more bloodshot. She admitted that she had had an attack of what she called stomach pains after lunch. Before leaving, he saw her back to her room. As soon as she sat down there she had another attack of the pain, which was evidently severe. She was embarrassed at her display of weakness and kept apologising to him. The attack passed and he gave her his blessing and left. The next day she seemed better and did not complain of any pains. She refused to let the nuns send for a doctor.

The following day, Friday 12 May, she spent the morning resting as usual in her room. After lunch she made her way again to the summerhouse and sat in the easy chair. Mother Arsenia had made some cushions for the chair to make it more comfortable. She had also just finished a new dress for Edel and she brought it out to her to make sure it fitted properly. Then one of Edel's priest friends, Father Butler, arrived and spent some time chatting to her before leaving. He noticed nothing wrong. Sister Servita was in the convent and she got the African houseboy, Remigio, to bring her out some refreshments. She took them gratefully and said in Swahili, 'Mzuri sana', which means, 'It's very good.' He went back to the convent, leaving her alone.

He returned to the summerhouse a little later, about 6.15 p.m., and found Edel unconscious in the chair. He ran first to Sister Servita and then to Mother Arsenia with the same message: 'The memsahib is dying.' They got to the summerhouse and saw that she had suffered a heart attack. Mother Arsenia, who was a nurse, examined her quickly and sent the sister back to the convent for some brandy and a cold towel. It was just at this point that Miss Gannon arrived for her usual evening visit. When she saw what had happened she drove off at once to fetch a priest and a doctor.

Meanwhile Mother Arsenia got Edel to drink a few drops of brandy and then put the cold towel over her heart. The sister brought a crucifix and two candles from the convent and put them on the table. While she was lighting the candles Mother Arsenia held the crucifix to Edel's lips so that she could kiss it. In a very short time Miss Gannon was back with Fathers Byrne and Fullen. Father Byrne had brought the holy oils with him and he administered the sacrament of extreme unction, anointing Edel on her on eyes, ears, mouth and hands.

She was conscious from time to time and asked more than once, 'What's wrong with me, Mother? I feel very sick.' Mother Arsenia said, 'Jesus is coming.' Then she asked her, 'Do you know me?' Edel gripped the nun's hand and murmured something that seemed to begin with 'm'. Then she said more clearly, 'Mother, Mother.' She looked at the candles that the sister had lighted and smiled two or three times.

They carried her into her room and laid her on the bed. She said 'Jesus' once and moved her head. Mother Arsenia again held the cross to her lips. Edel looked at her and repeated 'Jesus, Jesus'. Father Fullen held the Legion statue of Our Lady before her eyes while Father Byrne recited the prayers for the dying. Her breathing began to grow shorter and they could see that she was slipping away gently before their eyes. She appeared to be in no pain and she remained calm and peaceful up to the end. As her senses faded it seemed fitting that the last thing she touched was the cross of Christ, the last thing she saw was the image of his Mother, the last thing she heard was the sound of the prayer of the Church.

Two doctors arrived almost simultaneously, Dr Doyle and Dr Anderson. They examined her and pronounced her dead.

The sisters dressed her in the white habit of their congregation and laid her out again on the simple iron bedstead in her room. They joined her hands and wound her rosary beads around them and placed the crucifix behind her head. They brought armfuls of red and white flowers from the garden and strewed them all about her until only her face and hands were visible. Someone took a photograph. She looked peaceful and serene, all the lines of pain gone from her face.

The following day her remains were brought to the St Austin's Church and on the day after, Sunday 14 May 1944, she was laid to rest in the nearby cemetery, close to the grave of Bishop Shanahan. The attendance included Bishop Heffernan, more than twenty priests, and a great crowd of lay people of all ages and races. The Legion prayers were recited in English and Swahili as the body was brought to the grave. 'It was the biggest and most touching funeral I have ever seen,' wrote Father Culligan. 'I don't suppose any death that has occurred in East Africa, or any death likely to occur for a long time has evoked or will evoke such wide-spread and deep sorrow.'

The news came to Dublin in a telegram to Frank Duff. He got on his bicycle and rode the eight miles out to Monkstown. When the door was opened and Mrs Quinn saw him standing there, there was no need for him to say anything. She knew at once.

A crude wooden cross was placed over her grave with the inaccurate inscription 'Miss Ethel Quinn'. It was soon replaced by a more worthy memorial, a Celtic cross in white marble which still stands there. The form is Irish, the material African, recalling the country

where she was born and the continent where she died. On the shaft
of the cross is carved the Legion vexillum. The inscription beneath
reads:

EDEL QUINN
Envoy of the Legion of Mary
to East Africa from 30th October,
1936, to 12th May, 1944, on which
day she died at Nairobi.
She fulfilled this mission with
such devotedness and courage as to
stir every heart and to leave the
Legion of Mary and Africa itself for
ever in her debt. The Holy Father
himself paid tribute to her great
services to the Church.
Of your goodness, therefore, will
you give her generous remembrance
in your prayers.
R.I.P.

Sources

The main source for Edel Quinn's life is to be found in her letters. Apart from the collection of about sixty-five letters sent to Pierre Landrin, there are very few dating from her time in Ireland. Once she started on her envoyship, she wrote regularly to the Legion headquarters, to her family, to various friends in Ireland, and to priests, nuns and Legion officers in Africa. There are more than six hundred of these letters still surviving and they enable us to follow her movements in Africa in great detail.

In addition to her letters, two of her diaries have been preserved, one for 1937 and one for 1939, together with some retreat notes made at various times during 1943. A rather cryptic spiritual notebook has been lost but an authentic copy has been preserved. There are also copies of some other spiritual writings attributed to her but as they cannot be authenticated they have not been used in this book.

Another major source is the testimony given by witnesses for her canonisation process during the period 1963 to 1971. A total of 258 witnesses gave evidence about her, covering every period of her life from her childhood to her death. These testimonies, almost all of which were given in English, are available only in an Italian translation. For this book, they have been translated back into English by the author. This means that they regrettably do not give the actual words of the witness but only the sense.

A number of witnesses were interviewed on tape by Father Robert Bradshaw in the early seventies. Many of them had already given evidence for the process but they added a number of interesting details. The interview with Frank Duff is particularly useful. Mr Duff also wrote a short booklet about her life.

The writings of Mary Walls (Sister Mary Celestine) have been referred to in the text. Her booklet *I Knew Edel Quinn* and her unpublished French memorandum give a unique insight into Edel's spiritual development.

The biography of Edel Quinn written by Cardinal Léon-Joseph Suenens and published in 1953 is deservedly famous. It has been translated into many languages and has made her life-story known throughout the world. Apart from its many other merits, it uses interviews with people now dead and extracts from documents now lost.

The guardian of all Edel's papers and of many other documents, tapes and photographs connected with her life, is Father Anselm Moyniham, O.P. His assistance and advice has been invaluable. Without him this book could not have been written.